Finding Fulfilment

Finding Fulfilment

Eight Steps to Achieving Your Ultimate Potential

Liz Simpson

PIATKUS

Published in the UK in 2000 by
Judy Piatkus (Publishers) Limited
5 Windmill Street
London W1T 2JA
e-mail: info@piatkus.co.uk

For the latest news and information on all our titles,
visit our website at www.piatkus.co.uk

ISBN 0 7499 2143 9

This book has been printed on paper manufactured with
respect for the environment using wood from managed
sustainable resources

Labyrinth illustration on p. 65 by Zena Flax,
adapted from Sig Lonegren, *Labyrinths: Ancient Myths and
Modern Uses*
Typeset by Palimpsest Book Production Limited
Polmont, Stirlingshire
Printed and bound in Great Britain by
The Bath Press, Bath, Somerset

Contents

INTRODUCTION

*Life . . . is not the sum of what we have been, but
what we yearn to be.*

José Ortega y Gasset, twentieth-century Spanish writer and philosopher

Congratulations. You are about to take the first step on a
fascinating journey – one that, if you see it through to the
end, will change your life for ever. It is different from most
expeditions in that you do not need physical stamina,
money or provisions. For this journey you need travel no
further than your imagination, because the destination is
not a place but a state of being: the achievement of self-
fulfilment. It can be summed up as the satisfaction of
knowing that you are living out your ultimate potential –
your life's mission.

The journey takes the form of a labyrinth, which is both
an ancient tool for self-discovery and a metaphor for life
itself. The idea of working with the labyrinth visualisation,
which you will be using in this book, came to me serendipitously, as do many of the best creative ideas. I had been
researching labyrinths for a book on the relationships
between earth energies and our physical, mental, emotional
and spiritual wellbeing. As someone who works with
people, helping to move them from where they are in their

lives to where they want to be, I was at the same time looking for a way in which to uncover more readily the deeper
desires and life visions of my coaching clients. Too often I
was finding that we were spending many sessions working
on what they *said* they wanted to achieve, when in fact
their true passions lay elsewhere. It occurred to me that
presenting the labyrinth as a visualisation technique would
be of help here. I felt that, by encouraging my clients to
venture deep inside their souls right at the beginning of our
work together, this would move them forward more
quickly and more effectively than standard coaching
methods which work at a conscious level. So I devised the
eight-step labyrinth process, a slightly less symbolically
oriented version of which is presented in this book, and
discovered that it was hugely successful – getting right to
the core of what was important to my clients rather than to
some conscious 'wish list'.

I began to explore my own deep-rooted desires through
walking pavement labyrinths in churches and turf mazes (see
p. 24) as well as my own imaginary labyrinth. Throughout
history labyrinths have been used in a variety of ways,
among them to induce a state of calmness before entering a
place of worship. Whenever I am feeling stressed or worried
I take myself into my mental labyrinth, emerging within
minutes in a much calmer, more centred physical, mental and
spiritual state. And if I have a question for which I am
consciously unable to find an answer, in my imagination I
walk through the seven pathways until I reach the centre of
my labyrinth, from where I never fail to get the right
symbolic reply.

Like my coaching clients, your focus may be on:

- better physical and mental health
- more satisfying relationships
- greater confidence and self-esteem
- enhanced creativity
- business or educational success or

- simply the ability to take a more positive approach to life generally

Whatever it is, the eight-step process described in this book has been designed to help you achieve fulfilment in all these areas. Most importantly, it will help you rediscover the person you have always meant or yearned to be. The very fact that you have picked up this book means that your soul is telling you now is the time to proceed on the most important journey you are ever likely to make. And it is my privilege to act as your guide.

Asking Questions

Unlike many other self-help books which purport to offer you answers to whatever challenges you may be facing, *Finding Fulfilment* is concerned with helping you ask the right questions. It focuses on questioning for one simple reason: the more questions you ask, the greater the number of answers – and thereby options – you expose. Of these myriad options, only you will know which ones are acceptable to your life vision and values. But at least you will have plenty of probabilities to play with.

Unfortunately, we have grown up in a culture in which we expect our parents, teachers, religious leaders, doctors and self-proclaimed 'gurus' to fix our lives for us. But that's rather like going into a restaurant with a stranger and asking them to order your meal for you. How can anyone else possibly know what you want? Despite the huge range of guides and therapists who offer to direct your life for you, to tell you what to do and to try to help you avoid the pain that is so vital to our spiritual growth and development, we still experience a sense of incompleteness – like a gnawing toothache that won't go away. Some people call it 'the mid-life crisis', but nowadays this rite of passage is occurring among people in their twenties and thirties too. Two-and-a-half thousand years ago the wisdom and humility of Buddha acknowledged that his disciples had to walk the path themselves, with the Enlightened One acting purely as their guide – just as I will do for you.

Accustomed as we all are to a predominantly passive culture populated by expert 'fixers', it may feel a little uncomfortable to be guided towards asking more and more questions, rather than to seek answers directly, which is the focus of this book. What it encourages you to do is open your mind to the possibility that you have access to all that has ever been, is, or will be. The reason for this is explained in Chapter 2 when we explore the science of quantum physics, which demonstrates that everything in the universe is harmoniously inter-related.

Visualisation

The best way I have found to unlock the potential for happiness and fulfilment that lies within everyone is through the process of visualisation. Since the 1960s, when sports psychologists discovered that athletic performance could be improved by fully imagining the specific actions and thoughts linked to success, creative imaging or 'guided visualisation' has been recognised as a valuable technique for creating all sorts of changes in our lives. Doctors have used mental imagery, for example, as a tool with cancer patients: mutant cells are 'zapped' in the imagination as if they were aliens in a computer game, or bathed in love until they change form. Many of the more innovative experts within orthodox medicine are opening up to the value of using visualisation techniques to handle a variety of common ailments, too, such as speeding up the healing of wounds and curing sore throats. And you can do this for yourself, not only to deal with a wide range of illnesses, both minor and more serious, but, more importantly, to ensure that your body and mind are maintained in optimal health.

One UK psychologist even found that exerting mind over matter can strengthen muscles – handy for those of us with a loathing for gyms! In tests, students who engaged in exercises to strengthen their little finger got the same results as those who just imagined that they were doing them.

Visualising can seem like a very nebulous concept. This is not surprising since therapists who work with this amazing mental tool often give very little guidance on how to achieve the best results. Since you are reprogramming your future, you need to take the technique to its ultimate conclusion. For example, many people visualise an empty space when they want to park their car in a busy area. But I have never found this works for me. What I do is to visualise my car already parked there. As long as I conjure up a realistic picture in my mind, this is how I find rare parking spaces when everyone else complains about having to drive around for hours without such 'luck'.

When you come to visualise your future, see yourself enjoying the benefits of whatever it is you desire. Instead of visualising that you have just met the partner of your dreams, conjure up a picture of the two of you celebrating your golden wedding anniversary or (if marriage isn't important to you) still cuddling up together when you're retired. If you are suffering from a debilitating health problem, visualise yourself doing something which you cannot currently do because of your illness. Or, if your focus is on a more secure financial future, don't just picture yourself with a wad of cash which could get stolen, lost or be needed to pay bills. See yourself enjoying a better lifestyle, wearing designer clothes, living in a more attractive place and actively benefiting from that extra money.

If you have any doubts about the physiological and psychological power of your mind's eye, just conjure up a picture of someone you love deeply, or lust over, or with whom you have a difficult relationship. You will be able to observe immediate changes to your heartbeat, the amount of saliva you produce, the size of your pupils and your rate of breathing. Over the past forty years or so considerable scientific evidence has been adduced for this effect, as you will discover in Chapter 4 when the benefits of visualisation techniques are discussed in more detail. Remember that your brain, for all its complexity and brilliance, cannot distinguish what is real and what is realistically imagined. Through the techniques and exercises in this book, you will find out how to use this fact to create new realities for yourself.

Although there is a strong spiritual element to this book, I wanted it to appeal to as wide an audience as possible, not just those who have already 'bought into' metaphysical explanations for the way life is. Whether we like it or not, we are a product of our biology and culture. Anyone who has ever suffered, even temporarily, from depression or low self-esteem will know that you cannot just wake up one morning with a compelling vision and make it happen. For that reason Chapter 7 offers a variety of tools and techniques to help over-ride some of the disempowering biochemical processes and beliefs with which we are saddled. These will help you realistically to integrate the insights you will gain from the labyrinth into your everyday life.

The Divine Within

The term 'Higher Self' is used throughout this book. Expressing your Higher Self aligns you to the fact that you are a spiritual being in human form, not a human being trying to be spiritual. This is your connection to God, the Divine, Universal Consciousness or whatever term you are most comfortable with to describe the ineffable force which for millennia has guided and inspired humankind.

Our connectedness with the Divine or Higher Self through the process of journeying inwards or introspection – Plato called it 'Know thyself' – is a concept that has been articulated by many of the world's greatest prophets, philosophers and sages:

> *And when he was demanded of the Pharisees when the kingdom of God should come, he answered them*

and said, The Kingdom of God cometh not with observation: Neither shall they say, Lo here! or, lo there! for, behold, the Kingdom of God is within you.'

St Luke's Gospel 17:20–21

Self-knowledge is the shortest road to the knowledge of God.

Islamic sage

The Divine is not something high above us. It is in heaven, it is in earth, it is inside us.

Morihei Ueshiba, founder of Japanese martial art Aikido, which, translated, means 'The Art of Peace'

Buddhahood is the realm of the sacred knowledge found in oneself.

Zen Master Dahui

Here, in my own soul, the greatest of all miracles has taken place – God has returned to God.

Meister Eckhart, fourteenth-century Christian mystic

Humanistic psychologist Dr Abraham Maslow, generally acknowledged as one of the twentieth century's foremost experts on human behaviour and motivation, expressed this concept in terms of 'self-actualisation' – everything that one is capable of becoming. This highly regarded and influential expert on human behaviour and motivation formulated a hierarchy of needs in the shape of a pyramid: at its apex is the desire for self-fulfilment, in other words to live out one's potential. But don't think you have to reach the ultimate level of physical, financial and psychological security before being in a position to strive for more spiritual rewards. Down the centuries and across all cultures human beings have displayed an innate need to heed the call from within in order to experience the sacredness of their lives directly. Everyday life can be a spiritual practice, regardless of the constraints placed upon us by our circumstances.

Nor is Maslow's hierarchy necessarily the right way up – as the psychologist himself admitted just before he died. We all know that the basic needs of survival, safety, social belonging and self-esteem are only worth striving for when we have uncovered a deeper meaning, purpose and value in life. And every day we read stories in the press about individuals who, despite having had challenges to overcome, have chosen not to be victims and have achieved their dreams. Like the UK media mogul and multi-millionaire, Chris Evans, who was allegedly bullied at school because of his vivid ginger hair, spectacles, pale face and puny build. Or the award-winning actress, Tara Fitzgerald, whose father committed suicide when she was a child and who lived in squats with her mother and sister. Or the US government's highest-ranking woman, Madeleine Albright, whose Czech family had to flee from both the Nazis and the Communists during World War II. Or the UK's best-loved and most successful cookery writer, Delia Smith, who says she was a failure at school and that she had no self-confidence for years because of that unhappy experience.

The secret to finding fulfilment is embraced in three key universal laws around which the pathways of the labyrinth have been grouped:

- Dream
- Do
- Detach.

This means imagining the difference between where you are and where you want to be, taking the steps necessary to make that vision a reality, then learning to move aside and allow the universe to take care of the details – that is, not to place limitations on your life by becoming obsessed with achieving a specific outcome.

Whether you are comfortable with notions like the

Higher Self and tapping into Universal Consciousness, or whether you prefer a more scientifically based approach, doesn't matter. What both perspectives agree on is that the seeds of change must begin with self-awareness. The key is reflection, imagination, a heightened level of consciousness and the capacity to seek creative alternative solutions to life challenges through visualisation techniques, and challenging long-held assumptions.

Journey to the Centre of your Self

The ancient esoteric concept of the labyrinth has for thousands of years been regarded as a metaphor for life itself, as you will see from Chapter 1. Our ancestors knew how necessary it is to travel deep within ourselves to find our unique purpose and sense of satisfaction – in spiritual terms, to achieve enlightenment.

The labyrinthine 'map' offered in this book has been honed and refined until it represents the most effective tool I know with which to achieve your ultimate potential. I have also seen clients receive all some or of these knock-on benefits:

- As a tool for mental relaxation the labyrinth helps reduce stress levels and therefore guards against stress-related diseases
- By engaging both hemispheres of the brain, the labyrinth encourages lateral thinking and enhanced creativity
- The self-knowledge gained is invaluable because you will then know what kind of work, partnerships and friendships you want in your life, and as a result you will magnetically attract these aspirations into it
- When you see your life as a 'grand plan' which is unfolding gradually – like the labyrinthine pathways themselves – and not as a purposeless existence, it is easier to feel calmer, more trusting and optimistic about the future

- The increased confidence and self-esteem that come from experiencing life as an exciting, self-created adventure are likely to enhance the way you are regarded by others in your daily life, leading to greater social and career success now and in the future
- Best of all, you will see life as more fun and joyful

As the Greek philosopher Socrates advised: 'To find yourself, think for yourself.' To that I would add that the wisdom you will accrue as you work your way through this book requires a depth of thought which has long since ceased to be habitual in Western society. Don't be deceived into thinking that, among the various exercises I shall ask you to perform, those which require you to do little other than reflect and meditate will be the easiest. The mind is like a mine. While it is tempting just to collect whatever appears on the surface, it is from the greatest depths that you will eventually excavate the greatest treasures, and this requires patience, effort and courage.

In order to overcome life's challenges, remember the words of Buddha: 'We are what we think. All that we are arises with our thoughts. With our thoughts we make the world.' Then consider: what kind of world do you want for yourself? If the goal of self-actualisation, of rediscovering the sacred within, of finding your bliss and of living a life of potential greatness is compelling enough, you won't worry about the time, effort and challenges involved in this process – you will have your sights set only on the glittering prizes.

Bringing About Lasting Change

You may have come across books, workshops or training programmes that put forward techniques for making fundamental changes to the way you live, work and relate to others. Maybe, for you, they worked for a short time; but, even so, the chances are that within a few months you found things were little different from before. Rest assured, if you read this book carefully, and complete the exercises asked of you, you really will bring about lasting change and create a more fulfilling perspective to your life.

How to Use this Book

The eight-step process for finding fulfilment comprises seven pathways leading to the centre of the labyrinth, which is step eight. As mentioned earlier, each of the eight steps is grouped under the headings of Dream, Do and Detach, and each has its own visualisation element:

Dream Pathways

One: your future – the vision for your life

Two: tension – the difference between where you are and where you want to be

Three: detail – the new attitudes, beliefs, behaviours and values consistent with your future life

Do Pathways

Four: change – what you need to start doing differently to create your new reality today

Five: intuition – discovering the inner resources that will help you overcome current and future challenges

Six: diversity – your 'mystery mentor' who will guide and inspire you through these changes

Detach Pathways

Seven: the unknown – becoming open to new, unimagined possibilities by detaching from specific outcomes

Eight: destiny – the pool from which a symbolic gift awaits you to help you find fulfilment in your life.

You can use the eight-step labyrinth visualisation in a variety of ways:

- The first is through a mental pilgrimage, which is its principal focus
- The second is to find a labyrinth in a local church or public place and make arrangements to walk it over a specific period of time
- The third is to invest in your own permanent outdoor labyrinth, constructed with stones or cut into turf, or to make or buy a personal, portable canvas labyrinth that you can enjoy in the privacy of your own home or garden. See p. 177 for details of organisations that can help you choose

However, if you don't want to invest the time or expense in walking a tangible labyrinth, this book contains everything you need to benefit from this extraordinary spiritual tool. To enjoy the greatest advantage from this experience, irrespective of the actual method you choose, first read the book right through to understand the individual purpose of the eight pathways and how to integrate the insights gained into your life during the return journey and beyond. *Finding Fulfilment* has been written rather like a labyrinth itself; you will undoubtedly find something 'around the corner' that has a direct bearing on how you can best proceed.

Remember, the goal is not to work your way through this book as quickly as possible, but as thoroughly as possible. I have a poster on my study wall which reads 'Success is a journey, not a destination'; it reminds me to enjoy the process of life and not to miss out on its daily gifts by being too focused on my objectives. Without exception, each client or friend whom I have introduced to the eight-step labyrinth process has found that it helps them unleash their potential for a more successful and personally fulfilling life. That is partly because I have acted as life coach as well as tour guide for them, ensuring that every step, every piece of internal ground, is covered meticulously – from understanding the concepts presented to actually doing the exercises required.

But while I am with you in spirit as you work your way through this book, you are being called upon to act as your own coach, questioning your motives, offering unconditional support and pushing yourself that little bit further, harder and deeper. This involves a degree of persistence, courage, consistency and determination that is often easier to achieve when you have someone behind you saying:

- 'Do you *really* understand that concept?'
- 'Are you ready to take it on board emotionally, and not just intellectually?'
- 'When can you set aside enough time to complete that exercise?'
- 'Have you come up with authentic answers to those questions – replies that truly reflect your needs and not just the first thing that's come into your head?'
- 'What are you doing? Are you really pushing yourself to reach the glittering prizes or superficially playing at accessing your soul potential?'
- 'Don't you owe it to yourself to take time and effort over this, the most important journey you are ever likely to make?'

Doodling labyrinths is a wonderful way to relax the body, centre the mind and tap into your spirit. Become proficient with drawing the Classical Seven-circuit Labyrinth (see pp. 65) in order to discover the meditative blessings of creating them for yourself. For this mental pilgrimage you will need to create a black and white or coloured drawing that you feel happy working with. If you have a PC you may wish to produce a computer-generated illustration and then use your mouse or finger to trace the paths on screen.

Ideally ask a trusted friend – someone with a pleasant, soothing voice – to record the various guided visualisations on to one or more audiotapes. If this is not possible then you can record the tapes yourself, but it is much better and more effective to work with someone else's voice. See p. 73 for how to create your own visualisation audiotapes.

Although it will undoubtedly be tempting to enter the labyrinth with a specific question or issue in mind, the best results of this eight-step process are achieved when you free yourself mentally of such constraints. Frequently your Higher Self has a message for you that is quite different from the one that your conscious mind thinks it needs to address, because the Higher Self is operating from a deeper level.

The labyrinth is not a divinatory tool in the manner of runes, tarot cards or an astrology chart. Finding fulfilment is not about whether a particular partner will make you happy, but what you need to do to form an authentic relationship with yourself. Only then will you be complete enough to enter into a deeply satisfying relationship with another person. The journey is not about choosing one job over another but whether you are truly expressing your authenticity, passion and life purpose through your work. And if not, how you can. Nor is it about the quickest and easiest way of amassing a fortune, but how you can learn to respond to money as a source of energy that ebbs and flows like any other.

Basically, finding fulfilment is not about trying to

change other people or to control your environment (neither of which are possible and just waste your energy), but about completing yourself by rediscovering those parts of you that help you become a whole, centred and fully operational human being. Finding fulfilment means that all the day-to-day challenges that face you now will take on a different perspective. Every day of life is made up of happiness and sadness, pain and pleasure, dark and light, growth and decay in accordance with the ancient Chinese concept of Yin and Yang (see p. 29). It is not what happens to you but how you respond to what happens to you that will determine how joyous and fulfilling your life will be.

Set aside at least half an hour in which to engage in finger-tracing your labyrinth. Then begin working your way through the various exercises outlined in Chapters 4–7. These have been designed to help you understand and integrate into your life the divine messages from the labyrinth. Whenever you take a break, draw several labyrinths (see p. 65) and trace your finger along the pathways to centre and calm yourself again before doing further exercises. This is best done during the evening or just before you are going to settle down for the night and could become a ritualised activity involving lighting candles, burning incense, playing music or meditating.

Remember, it is not your conscious mind you are tapping into – you do that every day anyway. Each time you embark on one or more of the exercises you need to tweak the mental dial connecting you to your Higher Self.

The eight-step process prompts you to think about some of the issues that will be explored in the exercises in Chapters 4–7. I suggest you keep a journal handy in which you can note the thoughts, questions, pictures or other insights that come to you while journeying through the labyrinth. However, try to keep writing to a minimum during the journey itself (no more than a word or sentence for each pathway) because it engages the left, rational hemisphere of the brain too much and you want to be operating primarily on the right, creative side. This journal can include a record of the work you do on the subsequent exercises. It is also useful to keep this written record of your experience by your bedside so you can jot down any particularly vivid dreams that may symbolically contain messages of Divine Guidance. You mind will be extremely creative at this time – don't risk losing any of the nuggets of wisdom it releases.

Remember: spiritual development can be a fun, relaxing experience. Despite the feeling that you may be turning into a split personality, with mood swings from self-doubt to euphoria, enjoy yourself. I find it helpful to imagine I am the equivalent of Indiana Jones, a classical Greek hero like Theseus or Heracles or the intrepid Anglo-Saxon Beowulf and delight in the opportunity to take myself for a while out of my safe, suburban, twenty-first-century existence in order to have an adventure.

Above all, be kind, gentle and patient with yourself. No sensible navigator of challenging terrain would punish themselves unduly when physically, emotionally or mentally exhausted. Remember Aesop's fable of the tortoise and the hare.

The Tour Guide Has Been There Too

Have you ever visited a historic monument or stately home and had an official guide? Don't you find that some of them enhance the experience while others make you wonder why you bothered? Let's look at the difference between the two. First-hand experience of one's subject is essential, especially when the tour involves taking people into their inner self. It is termed 'walking your talk' – the demonstration that your companion not only knows her subject but has first-hand experience of it and can guide and empathise with you, as you undertake a similar journey, in a way that is not possible with only intellectual involvement.

The process described in this book is based not on theory but on a personal journey. I have walked every part of the labyrinth, becoming familiar with each twist and turn, each pitfall and pleasure. Having completed the journey for myself I now live a hugely fulfilled life doing work I love, magnetically attracting loving, supportive and inspiring people into my life, and enjoying the kind of successful and satisfying life that once I could only dream about.

The benefits of this process are physical, psychological and spiritual. I can honestly say that I have never felt more centred or purposeful or derived more fun, laughter and pleasure from life. Friends, particularly those who don't see me regularly, frequently say that despite the passing years I seem to be getting younger, both physically and energetically. But perhaps the most invaluable blessing I have received from my own foray into the labyrinth is to learn to trust. I now realise that in this jigsaw-puzzle existence we call life we may have all the pieces but not the picture on the box. All we can ever hope to do is trust that this picture – our life mission – is glorious, and keep reconstructing our lives accordingly. As an old Arab proverb enigmatically states: 'He who predicts the future lies, even if he tells the truth.'

It is my own experience and understanding of venturing into the imaginary labyrinth that qualifies me to guide you through your personal process and act as an empathetic and supportive companion. My own journey involved a lot of painful soul-searching, harsh lessons, temporary existential loneliness and the courage to confront my deepest fears – my 'Shadow' side (see p. 32). During my own labyrinthine process I cried oceans of tears, raged at what I perceived to be the unfairness of the world, trembled at my loss of 'control' and finally accepted that the Divine Plan – my destiny – is more glorious than anything I could have imagined for myself. The paradox of embracing both destiny and free will, and the reconciliation of the two, will become apparent as you work your way through this book.

Having come back out into the light, I can see much more

clearly that in my unwillingness to give up the life I thought I deserved I was in danger of sacrificing the life I was meant to have. And that life is one of immense happiness, self-fulfilment and satisfaction. When you emerge from the labyrinth it is as if you have been resurrected as the finest, most glorious, loving individual that you could imagine yourself to be.

This rebirth can only come from the death of the Lower Self or ego (which, as happiness expert Robert Holden suggests, is an acronym for Everything Good's Outside!). As countless spiritual teachers have emphasised, the door to a better life can only be unlocked from the inside. I know it to be true: I have travelled the subterranean labyrinthine recesses of my Higher Self and am living proof that the tears and tribulations are worth it. Read the comments of any heroic, enlightened human being who has faced life's challenges and they all say the same thing: that it was only by being placed into life's furnace and beaten into shape that caused their rough, original ore to be transformed into the most splendid gold filigree. That is why I call this an alchemical as well as a spiritual journey.

The Journey Ahead

Numerous mythological and fictional narratives demon-strate how much more painful life is for those who resist the Divine call to fulfil their destiny. In the Old Testament, the Book of Jonah is an allegorical tale of a man trying to avoid his destiny which, in his case, came as a direct communication from God. Told to go to Ninevah to act as a messenger of God, Jonah decided to opt out and flee to Joppa in order to find a ship to take him to Tashish instead. But the Divine is not so easily ignored and, when a great wind threatened to break up the vessel, Jonah was thrown into the sea by the mariners and swallowed by a giant fish. Only when he had repented, agreed to face his destiny and go to Ninevah was Jonah spat out on to dry land.

I have always considered Charles Dickens's *A Christmas*

Carol a splendid illustration of how, by changing our attitude, we can at any time change an undesirable destination. Scrooge asks the Ghost of Christmas Future: 'Are these the shadows of the things that Will be, or are they shadows of the things that May be, only?' Scrooge's destiny was meant to be very different from the self-destructive path upon which he was travelling because he had not yet found the power or spirit to do otherwise. It took a fearsome Spectre of the Future to terrify Scrooge – who, like most of us, was more afraid of the future than he was of the past or the present – into rediscovering the willpower to change his life, to become a complete human being with a heart and soul and not just a mind and body.

Please don't be one of those people whom fate drags along, kicking and screaming, rather than those who are led willingly to their destiny. In the end major illness, the messy break-up of a dysfunctional relationship, the loss of money or possessions will strip you spiritually naked and force you to reassess what is really important and where true fulfilment lies. You can make things easier for yourself by not resisting fate and venturing willingly into the labyrinth.

Are you now ready to begin searching for the hero or heroine within? Are you willing to prepare yourself for the exciting journey ahead – a journey towards wholeness and the realisation of your interconnectedness with all things?

> *However many holy words you read*
> *However many you speak*
> *What good will they do you*
> *If you do not act upon them?*
> Buddha

1

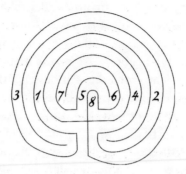

THE LABYRINTHINE JOURNEY

I want to know what sustains you from the inside when all else falls away. I want to know if you can be alone with yourself; and if you truly like the company you keep in the empty moments.

Oriah Mountain Dreamer, Native American Elder, May 1994

Now as I lie on my deathbed, I suddenly realise: If I had only changed myself first, then by example I would have changed my family. From their inspiration and encouragement, I would then have been able to better my country; and, who knows, I may even have changed the world.'

Inscription on the crypt of an Anglican bishop, Westminster Abbey

At some point in life you may feel totally alone – physically, psychologically and spiritually. As a teenager you probably suffered the angst of believing that no one else had ever experienced the pain of unrequited love; as an adult it is common to think that no one else can understand what life is like for us. Not only is this not true, but also the same quest for meaning, purpose and fulfilment has been a part of the human experience for millennia.

Uniting Body and Soul

The internal quest you are about to take is a pilgrimage as sacred as one made to Mecca, Jerusalem, Glastonbury or any other spiritual site. To undertake a pilgrimage at least once in life has been a driving force for countless individuals almost since the dawn of humankind, partly for physical healing but mainly to unite body and soul and to take part in a celebration of transforming the profane into the sacred.

The theme of merging is central to this book. If you look at the illustration on p. 20 you will see that the labyrinth loosely resembles the human brain, which is basically composed of two portions known as cerebral hemispheres:

- *The left hemisphere* is associated principally with mental activities such as logic, analysis, words, numbers, sequence and linearity
- *The right hemisphere* is dominant in spatial awareness, creativity, imagination, rhythm, colour and seeing the 'bigger picture' or organised whole (gestalt).

Some of the labyrinthine pathways shown on p. 20 go from left to right (the odd-number pathways 1, 3, 5 and 7) while others veer from right to left (the even-number pathways 2, 4 and 6). Your journey will engage both sides of your brain, representing a 'wholeness' that pure analytical or logical thought does not allow.

The next chapter explains how society is beginning to blend the different traditions and voices of ancient spiritual beliefs, Eastern insights, Western philosophy and modern science in order to produce a harmonious chorus. That chorus helps individuals to unite their scientific upbringing with their spiritual beliefs and to discover that science and spirituality are not mutually exclusive.

This chapter, meanwhile, explores the past and brings it up to the present, in particular how and why since the very earliest times the labyrinth has been a universal metaphor for the human journey through life. It also explains the psychological and spiritual necessity of coming face to face with what the great psychologist Carl Gustav Jung called the Shadow side of the Self. In addition this chapter looks at the importance of rediscovering the Goddess within (the 'feminine principle') and at how to achieve completion through balancing all these disparate parts of our Self.

A Symbol Across Culture and Time

The derivation of the word 'labyrinth' remains shrouded in mystery. Some writers believe that the term comes from the Greek *labyrinthos*, thought to be of Egyptian origin, while others relate it to the word for a double axe, *labrys*, the emblem of certain kings of Crete. This was considered a symbol of great importance in Minoan culture and is linked with its bull-worshipping cults, which ties in with the story of Theseus and the Minotaur (see p. 27).

The labyrinth is a prime example of what Jung termed 'collective consciousness', its motif being universally expressed by cultures separated by both space and time. Spiral designs were carved into rocks outside Neolithic burial chambers such as the Newgrange megalith in Ireland, which dates from 3500 BC. The floors of countless churches built during the twelfth century in Italy and France, such as Amiens, Bayeux and Chartres cathedrals, contain pavement labyrinths.

Carved into one of the walls of the ninth-century Lucca cathedral in Italy is a tiny labyrinth motif which worshippers could trace with their fingers. It is thought that its purpose was to help people become calm and centred before they went in to worship.

As far back as the Ice Ages our distant ancestors were venturing into the bowels of the earth into caves that resembled naturally formed labyrinths, and on their walls they painted astonishingly skilled and imaginative animal scenes. These sanctuaries, such as the ones found in the French Pyrenees, were often accessible only via low, narrow tunnels or over slippery, hazardous rocks. Some anthropologists suggest that these subterranean places were as sacred to Stone Age communities as cathedrals and temples are to us today. It was here, in these labyrinthine caverns deep in the earth, that our forebears may have ritually undergone a personal experience, a communion with nature, that caused them to reflect on the major philosophical questions that still beset us today – questions such as 'Where have I come from?' and 'What is the purpose of my life?'

Labyrinth in Lucca Cathedral

The mysterious Nazca lines of Peru, made famous by Erich von Däniken's book *Chariot of the Gods*, include labyrinthine figures of animals, insects and birds, some of which are hundreds of feet long and can only be appreciated from the air. The Hopi tribespeople of North America have a symbol known as Mother Earth which, in its circular form, is identical to the Classical Seven-circuit Labyrinth whose design you will be using for your journey. The Hopi carved this symbol on rocks and built models of it at their sacred sites, where the labyrinth represented the spiritual rebirth experienced while travelling along life's pathways.

For centuries the Classical Seven-circuit Labyrinth design has also been cut into turf or constructed with stones across Britain and Scandinavia. The greatest concentration of stone labyrinths can be found on the Scandinavian coast, on the borders of Sweden and Finland. And one of the most complex 'turf mazes' in England, known as Julian's Bower and cut into a hill near the village of Alkborough in the Humber valley, closely resembles the labyrinth found in the nave of Chartres Cathedral. Labyrinth author and historian W. H. Matthews relates the custom of Welsh shepherd boys in the nineteenth century who would cut a labyrinthine figure into the turf of the fields in which they were working. This tradition may have started with the legend of Brutus and his prisoners from Troy – the reason why labyrinths cut into turf in Britain are sometimes referred to as Troy Towns or Walls of Troy. According to this legend, Brutus, a descendant of Homer's hero, Aeneas, came to Wales and brought with him a number of former prisoners from the Trojan War. Together they built a city on a hill which they named Caerdroia, meaning City of Troy (from *caer* = hill and *droia* = Troy). *Caerdroia* is the Welsh word for a labyrinth. (Alternatively, turf mazes may simply have been meant as a large-scale puzzle or game to alleviate the boredom of having nothing to do all day but watch sheep!) There is a subtle difference between a labyrinth and a maze (see p. 27).

Labyrinths were a recurring form in ancient art, featured on coins from the Minoan culture (the Cretan Bronze Age, lasting from approximately 2500 BC to 1200 BC), early Egyptian amulets, Bronze Age pottery and other artefacts. They are highly reminiscent of mandalas, symbols used by Buddhists to aid meditation and to find a spiritual focus, and as such illustrate a potential avenue from the profane to the sacred. The spiralling design of the labyrinth is also suggestive of kundalini energy, which, according to Hindu tradition, rises up through metaphysical energy centres known as chakras, piercing each in turn, until – arriving at the crown – the subject is said to have achieved enlightenment.

The Power of Seven

Some commentators relate the Classical Seven-circuit Labyrinth to the seven major chakras, each of which is linked to a colour of the rainbow as well as having a specific resonance. Like Maslow's hierarchy of needs mentioned on p. 7, the seven chakras relate to specific life topics starting with physical survival and working up to spiritual enlightenment. These issues can also be used to focus the mind on your particular life challenges in order to receive the intuitive wisdom to help overcome them. The traditional associations are:

Pathway	Chakra	*Colour*	Life topic
1	Root/base	*Red*	Survival/physical needs
2	Sacral	*Orange*	Emotions/sexuality
3	Solar plexus	*Yellow*	Personal power/self-will
4	Heart	*Green*	Love and relationships
5	Throat	*Blue*	Self-expression
6	Third eye	*Indigo*	Intuition/wisdom
7	Crown	*Violet*	Spirituality

If you look at the illustration of the Classical Seven-circuit Labyrinth on p. 20 and trace your finger along the numbered pathways, you will discover that, despite starting out halfway into the labyrinth, the earlier pathways (1, 2 and 3) move you right out to the perimeter. This is analogous to achieving your goals in life. While your early efforts may seem to take you further away from your centre – the ultimate goal of inner fulfilment – faith, perseverance and continuing to take steps into the labyrinth ensure that your goal will eventually be met. As in life, there is a need to keep covering 'old ground', each time from a slightly different angle or perspective, before the road appears to be moving you on.

Labyrinths are expressed in many different sizes and degrees of complexity and ornateness. The Classical Seven-circuit Labyrinth that we shall be using, as opposed to the more ornate Gothic motif found at Chartres Cathedral, is formed from seven concentric pathways with a centre. This centre contains the solution to your current life challenges as well as housing the treasure of self-fulfilment.

The number seven has many connotations. Mystics have long considered it a 'special' number. It is the sum of four and three, both of which were considered by disciples of the Greek mathematician Pythogoras to be particularly lucky. The following are just some of the other concepts with which the number seven is associated:

- deadly sins
- wonders of the ancient world
- chakras in the classical Hindu system of health and wellbeing
- ages of man
- virtues
- days in which God created the universe
- Churches of Asia – Ephesus, Smyrna, Pergamos, Thyatira, Sardis, Philadelphia, Laodicea
- gifts of the Holy Spirit (wisdom, understanding, counsel, fortitude, knowledge, righteousness, fear of the Lord)
- gods of luck in Japanese folklore
- a seventh son of a seventh son is said to have special occult powers
- we talk about being in 'seventh heaven', meaning supremely happy – an allusion to the seven heavens of the Kabbalists, the ultimate of which is the abode of God

The Difference Between a Labyrinth and a Maze

Most people's knowledge of labyrinths hinges on reading the Greek myths of Theseus and the Minotaur. As the story goes, Theseus was charged with killing this monstrous half man, half bull, the result of King Minos' wife's obsession and sexual coupling with a magnificent white bull that had been given to the king by the sea god Poseidon. For everyone's safety the Minotaur had been housed in a tomb-like maze of baffling complexity in the Palace of Knossos. In order to avenge his son Androgeos, gored to death by a bull in Athens, Minos ordered the Athenian King Aegeus to send seven of that city's young men and women to Crete every nine years to be sacrificed to the Minotaur. Theseus, the adopted son of King Aegeus, insisted on being one of the fourteen victims on the third occasion of this deadly tribute.

With the help of one of Minos' daughters, Ariadne, whom he had seduced, Theseus used a ball of thread to trace his journey to the centre of the maze, where he killed the Minotaur. All he had to do then was rewind the thread to find his way out.

In fact, what this myth describes is not a labyrinth but a maze, and these concepts are frequently muddled. While we shall be focusing only on the Classical Seven-circuit Labyrinth in this book, mazes are indeed relevant to the way some people regard their journey through life. They have many paths, some of which are dead ends and require the navigator to retrace his or her steps many times. Their construction is so tortuous that it often seems impossible to find the way to the centre, or the way back out again.

Hence mazes are the basis of many mentally stimulating games, since the need for cunning to solve them engages the logical mind. If you are puzzled by life and view it as being full of frustrations, red herrings, broken promises and the constant need to retrace your steps with no guarantee that you will ever make progress, then you are viewing it as analogous to a maze. You may be operating mainly from the left, logical side of your brain. Because life appears to offer no rational meaning, you are inclined to opt for a more negative interpretation of your personal journey.

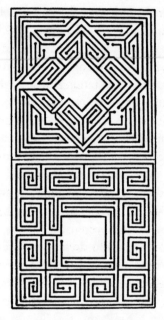

Mazes by G. A. Boeckler, 1664.

Labyrinths are also challenging, but because they consist of only one – albeit twisting and winding – path, it is persistence and blind faith that you need in order to reach the centre. Journeying through the labyrinth is analogous to the turning points that we face in life. While our destiny is represented by a single pathway, how we choose to walk it – fast or slowly, positively or negatively, with our focus on the goal we desire or allowing ourselves to get mixed up in other people's goals – involves our free will.

Yin, Yang and Balance

The myth of Theseus and the Minotaur includes a key theme which permeates this book. It is that of finding completion through realigning the masculine and feminine within the Self, a concept which the ancient Chinese termed Yin and Yang.

In many creation myths, such as the Chinese tale of the Cosmic Egg, it was written that the universe was created from both light and dark, the philosophical polarities of Yin and Yang, without which life as we know it would not exist. The labyrinth represents Yin, which stands for darkness, negativity and the feminine principle. According to this legend, before the world was formed there was only chaos in the shape of an egg, inside which were contained the opposing forces of Yin and Yang. Yin embodies the feminine principle, coldness, wet, darkness and passivity or negativity, while Yang contains the complementary forces of masculinity, heat, dryness, light and activity or positivity. However, this is not to suggest that ancient Chinese culture was misogynistic. The concept of Yin and Yang was conceived by the ancients as a dynamic phenomenon in which an individual who was centred and whole, regardless of gender, would fully experience the interplay of both masculine and feminine elements within themselves.

Similar to the Big Bang theory of twentieth-century physics, one day – so the story goes – these polarised energies began to fight within the cosmic egg, tearing it apart. Those elements that were heavy became compressed to make the earth, while the lighter ones floated around it and formed the sky.

The concept of Yin and Yang is traditionally depicted as an egg shape split into a dark side with a small circle of light and a light side with a small circle of darkness, demonstrating that there is no 'absolute' reality. The ancients believed it was the interplay of Yin and Yang that explained the continuing cycle of night and day, the changing seasons and the emergence of new life from the mingling of male and female. Without death we could not appreciate life, without activity we could not value stillness, and without rain and sunshine we would never know the glories of the rainbow.

The Yin Yang Symbol

Similarly, our lives as human beings can only become balanced and fortuitous when we honour both the conscious and unconscious forces at work in our lives. While we operate principally in the light, we need from time to time to venture into the darkness of the labyrinth in order to become truly whole.

Western patriarchal society favours and rewards competitive, aggressive, analytical, demanding male characteristics (Yang) at the expense of responsive, cooperative, intuitive Yin attributes. In order to bring about a fusing of light and dark, the conscious and the subconscious, the realms of the physical and the unmanifest or spiritual, at some stage in your personal evolution you must walk the non-rational, intuitive, meditative path of the labyrinth to help you become whole. Such an introspective journey is required because the Higher Self has become obscured by the ego or personality, like precious metals buried under centuries of mud and rock.

In Hindu philosophy this unifying principle or reconciliation of opposites is explained as the merging of existence (*sat*), consciousness (*cit*) and bliss (*ananda*). The Hindu texts known as the *Upanishads* talk about the relationship of the human soul or Self (*Atman*) and the Supreme Being (*Brahman*) as being like salt in water – each pervades the other. Hence our ultimate reality is to recognise that the individual Self and World Soul are one and the same and to strive for a new, empowered, though ineffable, state of consciousness – to know that we are one with *Brahman* and can reach the Supreme. This is consistent with what scientists have discovered about quantum reality, which is discussed in Chapter 2.

CASE HISTORY: Terry's Story

Terry's dream seemed to have come true. An unexpected legacy meant he could give up his humdrum job and realise a lifelong passion to write the novel that had been playing around in his head for years. While it wasn't a fortune, the money was enough to allow him to concentrate on writing for the next year or so.

Terry had the vision, the self-belief and now the financial security with which to make his dream a reality. But something was wrong. He found it difficult to motivate himself, and the little work he did produce was stale and uninspired. When several standard coaching sessions failed to get to the root of the problem, I invited Terry to venture into his personal labyrinth.

As I guided him through each of the imaginative pathways, a recurring theme presented itself – another Terry popped up, someone who looked exactly like him but was more powerful, aggressive, 'baser' and with an uncontrollable passion. I suggested that he asked this 'second self' to accompany him on the rest of the journey. But first, Terry had to find out what would motivate his companion to do so. Terry intuited that this dark shadowy figure wasn't interested in Divine Guidance or messages from his Higher Self, but only in 'crass desires' like money and fame. Once Terry was assured that his Shadow would find fulfilment in whatever form suited him best, both Terrys continued on their journey.

In the centre of the labyrinth something wonderful happened. In his mind's eye, Terry became aware of a blinding white light which enveloped him and his companion, blending them together. On the journey out of the labyrinth Terry was troubled by this, believing he had got the best part of the deal. While merging with his Shadow – all the parts of himself that Terry feared or disliked most – offered him the power, primal edge and passion with which to fuel his creativity, he felt a sense of betrayal for his darker side.

One of the exercises Terry agreed to engage in after the journey was to befriend his Shadow, to get to know and accept this materialistic, 'baser' side of himself. In the weeks that followed Terry discovered a drive and creative edge to his work that had been missing before. Far from being a negative, materialistic force, his Shadow helped him put a monetary value on his time and efforts and to see that pursuing a creative career didn't mean he had to forgo material aspirations. Terry also recognised that, far from betraying his Shadow, it was only through engaging with his more civilised, reasonable and socially acceptable counterpart that the Shadow could best express his gifts.

Terry's experience demonstrates how, once we have found the courage to face and get to know our Shadows, they are nothing to fear. They provide us with different facets of ourselves which enable us to become complete, fully functioning human beings. Working with his Shadow, and not trying to suppress him, Terry became the compelling, strong, impassioned writer that he had always longed to be, but was afraid would be unacceptable to others. When blended, both sides of Terry were perfect, each finding fulfilment according to his specific needs.

EXERCISE: Benefiting from your Shadow

One of the ways our Shadows seem to be at their most debilitating is when they dominate our thoughts. Their negative influence can sometime overwhelm and under-mine our positive and empowering Self, but both have their part to play in moving you from where you are to where you want to be. To demonstrate this for yourself, try the following exercise. It is also a powerful mood-breaker, so use it whenever you want an effective way to overcome negative feelings.

Take a large sheet of paper and head it with whatever put you in your negative mood, such as:

- 'My friend has let me down again.'
- 'No one loves me.'
- 'I can't cope by myself.'
- 'I deserved that promotion – it's not fair that I didn't get it.'

Underneath that heading make two columns, the left one marked 'Unreasonable thoughts' and the right one 'Realistic thoughts'. Now just start to write, without judg-ing or editing them in any way, all your thoughts about the situation that you are allowing to affect you so much, pair-ing them up as appropriate. Here's one example:

Negative belief:
I will never find a partner I want to spend the rest of my life with.

Unreasonable thoughts	**Realistic thoughts**
There's no one out there for me.	But I've had lots of fulfilling partnerships – just not 'The One' That doesn't mean he/she isn't out there, just that we've not met yet.
I only attract people I'm not really interested in.	Is that really true? And even if it were, at least those experiences are helping me discover what really attracts and works for me.

Lovers never seem to want to commit.	So why would I want to be with someone like that? Think of it as a lucky escape.
All the people I meet are so shallow.	Maybe I'm looking in the wrong places. Why not widen my social circle a bit? Use what I know about what I want in a partner to work out the kind of environment/social situation in which I'm most likely to find them.
Either they get fed up with me or the other way round. Nothing seems to last.	Maybe I don't want one partner for the rest of my life. Where did that idea come from? Do I really believe that a lifelong commitment is the ideal situation for me?

This exercise has two benefits. First, the act of writing your thoughts down automatically helps to lift your mood. Secondly, you discover that for every negative thought there is a positive one that can help shift your thinking and/or cause you to change your behaviour to be more empowering, such as deciding to look for a potential partner in a different social environment. When something isn't working, this is the catalyst for change. By doing something to confront the negatives in your life, you are motivated to live more positively.

The Goddess within

If you look at the Yin–Yang symbol on p. 30 you will notice that within the Yin there is a dot of Yang and vice versa. Similarly, whichever gender you are, there is a need to recognise and celebrate the Divine Feminine within. Because they represented the Divine in nature to cultures which worshipped one or more female deities, labyrinths have come to be associated with the Divine Feminine. This is not surprising, since walking a labyrinth, mentally or physically, is about getting in touch with your intuitive, nurturing, consolidating Yin energy.

Just north of the thirteenth-century walled city of Visby in Sweden is a place called Galgberget, which contains one of that country's best-preserved labyrinths. Here, as throughout Scandinavia, according to mythology a woman resides at the centre of the labyrinth. In some stories, as with the one connected with Galgberget, she is held prisoner but eventually released; in others, she is the prize to be won by whichever male gets to the centre fastest or without stumbling. This concept is linked to the story of the Trojan War (see p. 24), which was fought over the beautiful Helen. The myth of Theseus and the Minotaur (see p. 27), while telling of a half male/half monster figure at the centre of the labyrinth, also contains a strong female element. Both Pasiphae, Minos' wife and daughter of the Sun, and their daughter Ariadne have divine connections and in the female-oriented Minoan culture were linked with the worship of the Mother Goddess. As author and labyrinth expert Sig Lonegren explains, the patriarchal Greeks may have rewritten an older version of the Minoan story, in which the Goddess and not a monster was met at the centre of the labyrinth, to suit their own cultural discrimination against women.

In many fairy stories a prince (representing the Freudian psychoanalytical concept of the 'animus' or masculine principle) battles his way through the labyrinthine corridors of a castle or a similarly tortuous wood in order to reach his princess, representing the female 'anima'. These archetypal stories illustrate the importance of the coming together of both sides of one's psyche, masculine and feminine. It was thought that venturing into the labyrinth allowed a person to reclaim the previously lost female side of themselves.

The six-petalled rosette at the centre of more ornate labyrinths, such as that on the floor of Chartres Cathedral is, according to Dr Lauren Artress, redolent of the goddesses Isis and Aphrodite or Venus – the rose being a symbol of beauty and of Divine as well as human love. And the *labyrs* or double-axe symbol which can be seen at each turn on these kinds of labyrinth is said by the same author to be traditionally viewed as a symbol of female power and creativity. The twenty-eight lunations or curvatures on each quadrant of the perimeter of the Chartres labyrinth are thought to be linked with the lunar calendar. Again, the moon in mythology was known in the various female forms of Hecate, Ashtaroth, Diana, Selene and Phoebe.

In the Greek myth of Theseus it is only with female help that the hero accomplishes his mission. Like Ariadne's thread, our link with the Divine is gossamer-like in its subtlety but nevertheless maintains an unbreakable connection between our internal and external realities. It is essential to both sexes to get in touch with their feminine side and so become whole again. This is the key to finding fulfilment and the focus upon which this eight-step labyrinthine process has been developed.

Churches and Christianity

As mentioned earlier, labyrinths – despite having their origins in pre-Christian cultures and times – were integrated into the walls and floors of medieval churches. That a non-Christian symbol should appear in such places of worship is not so surprising, because the only way the Christian Church could overcome millennia-old pagan beliefs and traditions was to build its houses of God on top of heathen sites. In addition the Christian Church adopted pagan festivals (including the Winter Solstice, which became 'Christmas') and adapted customs such as bobbing for apples and Easter egg hunts. The latter bear no relation to Jesus Christ's resurrection but came about in honour of the pagan Mother Goddess in order to celebrate the earth's fertility and the new life born in the spring. Even the word 'Easter' is of pagan origin, derived from the Germanic goddess of fertility, Eostre. As you can see from the illustration on p. 66, the Classical Seven-circuit Labyrinth is based on a cross shape, although this has nothing to do with Jesus Christ; it traditionally represented the traveller's connection with nature through the four points of the compass. Seventeenth-century woodcuts by the Danish antiquary Olaf Worm depict a labyrinth symbol engraved on an ancient cross, but there is no known reason why this should be so, except that the labyrinth motif is a common feature among Nordic tribespeople.

Labyrinth in Chartres Cathedral

Various theories have been proposed as to why labyrinth markings have been found so extensively in European churches. Some say that the labyrinth was a symbol of Christian life with its twists and turns. Others hold that pavement labyrinths were a miniature substitute for pilgrimages, particularly for the very young, old or infirm who could not travel far. One writer even suggests that the average two hours spent on one's knees going around a typical pavement labyrinth represented the length of time it took for Jesus Christ to journey from Pontius Pilate's house to Calvary.

However, the practice of assimilating the female-inspired archetypal symbol of the labyrinth into Christian churches highlights a bitter irony. The institutionalised distrust of women that pervaded the Catholic Church for hundreds of years resulted in vicious witch-hunts. Hundreds of thousands of people, 95 per cent of whom were women, were burnt, drowned or otherwise murdered – and all for actions no more sinister than those undertaken by contemporary midwives, herbalists and astrologers.

The Loss of Labyrinths

Religious worship of the Great Goddess (or, as some contemporary archaeologists and anthropologists believe, female deities who were honoured in addition to their male counterparts) predates all three patriarchal Western religions – Christianity, Islam and Judaism – by thousands of years. Numerous cultures worldwide, including the Minoans, the ancient Egyptians and the early Britons, worshipped the Divine Feminine as well as male gods. Pagan practices such as Wicca celebrate the feminine principle within nature. Interestingly, the word 'witch' derives from the Anglo-Saxon word 'wicce' meaning 'wise one', a person who understands and works with divine forces. The deity of Wicca's followers is not some vengeful male God sitting on a cloud in a place inaccessible to living humans that Christians call Heaven, but a nurturing mother who envelops us daily. Pagans revere both the feminine and masculine principles – the Yin and the Yang – which make life whole and complete.

Over time, however, the tribes which understood this intrinsic balance in nature were taken over by Indo-Europeans whose chief deity was the fierce, warrior-like sun god. The newcomers' mythological tales began to undermine the female contribution to life by promoting other major gods such as the aggressive, cruel, unfaithful rapists Zeus and Poseidon. In the Bible it is clearly implied that the downfall of humankind rests on the shoulders of the apple-eating Eve. Hence not just women but their natural attributes of nurturance, intuition and creativity were subjugated and – because the male-only worshippers were not in touch with the feminine part of themselves – feared.

As mythological tales promoting the supremacy of gods over their female counterparts prevailed, our earth –

traditionally represented for millennia as the Mother Goddess Gaia – began to be plundered and raped for its resources, without thought to the resulting damage to the delicate cycle of the ecosystem. Humankind, particularly in the rational-obsessed West, became alienated from the Yin, not appreciating that by doing so it was creating a spiritual vacuum and natural imbalance from the way life is meant to be.

The disappearance of labyrinths as a spiritual tool came about as humankind was encouraged to turn away from the feminine principle symbolised by the pagan Goddess and focus on the reasoning mind and physical evidence. This is why, for centuries, countless individuals have found that their more spiritual, intuitive side has gone into hibernation.

Completion through Balance

As within nature, there is a delicate balance for humankind to achieve within ourselves. Although early civilisations such as the Minoans concentrated on a Great Goddess, Neolithic and later cultures worshipped many gods of both sexes. The multi-faceted relationships between these divinites are illustrated by mythological tales which portray them simultaneously as siblings, parents and consorts.

Some deities, like the Egyptian creator god Atum, represented both masculine and feminine principles and gave birth to their progeny by themselves – in this case, the twins Shu (god of air) and Tefnut (goddess of moisture). Twin births are a common theme in mythology, highlighting the Yin–Yang duality of equal yet opposite forces in nature. In the Greek pantheon, Artemis and Apollo are twins – she the moon, he the sun. In other examples, such as the Egyptian myths, we find sibling-consorts Osiris and Isis alongside their less well-known Shadow archetypes, Set and Nephthys. In later writings, twins have symbolically represented good and evil as in Alexandre Dumas's classic tale *The Man in the Iron Mask*.

Both male and female, light and shadow, positive and negative were honoured by our ancestors because, like the Yin–Yang symbol, polar opposites cannot exist without each other. We can learn much from our forebears' wisdom. Placing emphasis on the Divine Feminine through venturing into the labyrinth does not mean negating the importance of the masculine. Both sexes can benefit greatly from balancing the female and male aspects of their psyches. Nor should the concepts of 'male' and 'female' be confined to stereotypes. The ancient Greeks appreciated the diversity found within the sexes as well as between them, which is why a god like Apollo was portrayed as a *kourotroptoi* or nurturer, while Athena was a warrior-like, strategically minded, independent goddess.

Back to the Future

Today there is a resurgence of interest in labyrinths as we rediscover the eco-friendly, spiritually enhancing traditional knowledge of our ancestors – the 'baby' thrown out with the bathwater during the seventeenth-century Age of Reason and the resulting obsession with dominating our earth. Many contemporary organisations (see p. 177 for a list) are helping to facilitate the walking of labyrinths by organising tours to medieval churches with pavement labyrinths, as well as integrating portable canvas labyrinths into places of worship, be they Christian, pagan or New Age. In his cultural and historical analysis of labyrinths, Jacques Attali reports that a San Diego prison visitor takes a portable labyrinth with her for prisoners to walk; that several universities in California provide labyrinths for students to walk before their exams; and that an acute-care hospital in San Francisco has an outdoor painted labyrinth for use by staff, patients and their families.

If you do get the opportunity to walk a pavement or canvas labyrinth I highly recommend that you take it, particularly if there are other people on the pathways at the same time. How you manage this experience can highlight how you handle relationships of all kinds or even just relate to people generally.

CASE HISTORY: Marie's Story

While walking a pavement labyrinth in a cathedral in France, Marie was appalled to see people jostling each other, obviously frustrated or irritated at being held up by others who were in their opinion 'too slow'. With enough personal development behind to her to know that whatever provokes a strong reaction in you about other people's attitudes highlights a need to confront and resolve something similar in yourself, Marie considered her own thoughts and actions. With a little coaching she recognised how, especially at work, she got aggravated when her colleagues did not adhere to her personal timetable for getting things done. This was making Marie unpopular in the office.

Close friends (myself included) found the courage to stop withholding observations we had wanted to share with Marie for some time. Warm and wonderful as she was, we agreed that Marie was extremely judgemental about other people and would frequently berate, rather than support, friends who took longer to do things than she did. On one occasion Marie had almost fallen out with a long-standing girlfriend (a freelance journalist) by haughtily exclaiming that if she worked a lot harder and faster she would earn more money and wouldn't need to keep borrowing from other people. The truth, not revealed until later, was that this friend was working as hard and fast as she was able, but had been diagnosed with ME (myalgic encephalomyelitis, a post-viral syndrome resulting in chronic fatigure). Having suffered in silence for many years this friend needed support and compassion, not to be judged because she was less able.

By walking the labyrinth, with no particular thought other than to benefit generally from the experience, Marie learned an invaluable lesson about the way she related to others. It wasn't too long before both her working and personal life changed for the better as a result of these insights. She had found her own example of fulfilment.

Walking your Talk

Some people, having reached the centre of a pavement or canvas labyrinth, cross straight over to the outside without bothering to retrace their steps. But taking your time to reflect on the insights gained from the labyrinth during the return journey helps you integrate that learning into your everyday life. Chapter 7 covers this important point in more detail.

Other people enter the labyrinth and, because they are expecting some momentous 'Road to Damascus' experience, come away disappointed. They have not realised that, because they were focused on future expectations, they were never fully present and so were unable to receive the gift that Divine Guidance wanted to offer them.

Physically walking a labyrinth with other people highlights how you walk your path through life and in particular how you honour other people's journeys. However, you can also gain invaluable insights about yourself from tracing the labyrinth with your finger. Turn to p. 20 and move your finger along the labyrinthine pathways of the illustration. How did you find the experience? For example:

- Did this exercise force you to slow down physically and/or mentally?

- Did you find that the quicker you tried to trace the pathways the more likely you were to slip over the dividing lines?

- Did you have to change the angle of your finger in order to 'see' where you were going?

- Was it easier to keep your finger perpendicular and look directly down on the labyrinth in order to maintain control of the overall process? What does this suggest about taking a bird's-eye view of life?

- If you tried to look too far ahead, did you lose your way off the path you were on, demonstrating the importance of being 'present' at all times on your own life path?

- How much time did you spend in the centre?
- Did you immediately trace your way back out?
- Was going into the labyrinth easier for you than coming out?
- Did you have to change anything in order to make the reverse journey easier to trace?

Now relate how you undertook this exercise to the way you make your way through life. What insights has this thrown up for you?

Onwards and Downwards

Eager as I am sure you are to embark on your journey, understanding *why* the eight-step process works, in line with current understanding about our quantum reality, will enhance your experience by answering some of the doubts common to those of us who are steeped in rational thought and mechanistic ways of living. As a means of stepping into your future, let's now explore some more. . . .

2

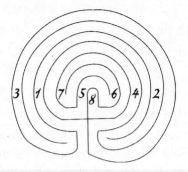

THE INTERNAL LOCK

What lies behind us and what lies before us are tiny matters compared with what lies within us.

Ralph Waldo Emerson, nineteenth-century American writer

Mind and matter no longer appear to belong to two fundamentally separate categories, as Descartes believed, but can be seen to represent merely different aspects of the same universal process.

Fritjof Capra, physicist and author of books on the philosophical implications of modern science

When our ancestors decided they wanted to create a spiritual tool as a metaphor for life's journey, why did they not just draw a straight line? Why a curving, winding labyrinth? The reason is that life is not the linear passage that our mechanistic, Newtonian inheritance would have us believe. Financial markets operate in a cyclical fashion, rather like the seasons, with 'bull' markets followed by 'bears' and vice versa. Careers are rarely experienced as a direct path from college to retirement, especially nowadays when each of us is likely to have four or five different types of employment in the course of our working lives and 'portfolio careers', with many, varied sources of income coming from several jobs undertaken simultaneously are increasingly common. The most successful commercial organisations, such as 3M, Sony and Disney, didn't hit upon one product or service and stick with it throughout their history, but diversified in order to offer the market what it wanted and needed next.

The Cosmic Web

The evidence that ours is not a linear existence has been around us all along. We live in a solar system whose planets travel along elliptical pathways orbiting the sun, just as subatomic particles spin around a nucleus. Curves and spirals are abundant throughout nature, from the way plants unfurl themselves as they grow to the shape of sea shells. Recent experiments in which sound is passed through sand and other malleable material demonstrates that harmonics produce waves, spirals and circular shapes. The sacred syllable *om*, intoned as part of Hindu contemplation and devotion, has been found to produce a vibrational image of concentric circles.

And now, at last, we are able to prove what the ancients knew intuitively – that the universe is a cosmic web of dynamic, interconnecting patterns and forms representing both change and continuity. The Neo-Confucian Wang Yang-ming (1472–1529) put it this way: 'That the great man can regard Heaven, earth and the myriad things as one body is . . . because it is natural with the humane nature of his mind that he should form a unity. . . '. The proof comes thanks to developments in quantum physics, fractal mathematics and chaos theory – the sciences of pattern, probability and paradox.

At a subatomic level there is no 'reality', just a tendency for things to exist as either concrete, physical matter or fields of invisible energy, according to whatever they are forced to interact with. It is how an experiment is set up, and the expectation of the experimenter, that determines whether he observes particles of matter or waves of energy.

Hence, at the most basic level of life, things do not exist independently but only in terms of their relationship with other things. This led leading quantum physicist Werner Heisenberg to say: 'The world thus appears to be a complicated tissue of events in which connections of different kinds alternate or overlap or combine and thereby determine the texture of the whole.' This will be an important point to remember when you discover why the eight-step process labyrinth process works.

Modern science, then, is the science of pattern, highlighting the complexity of life which operates under a completely different set of principles from the ordered, controllable 'rules' that orthodox science has hitherto sought to identify and predict. Paradoxically, this shadow nature of physical reality is closer to the metaphysical or mystical view of the world which our earliest ancestors embraced. Science and spirituality have been blended by some of the greatest scientific philosophers of modern times, including David Bohm, Albert Einstein, Carl Gustav Jung, Robert Jahn and Brenda Dunne of Princeton University (see p. 131) and Fritjof Capra. For them, science and spirituality have ceased to be mutually exclusive.

Sacred Geometry

Thousands of years ago our ancestors worked in harmony with nature through geomancy – the fusion of many subjects including sacred geometry, ecology, architecture, harmonics and music, astronomy and cosmology. Geomancy (its prefix geo- is derived from the name of Gaia, the Greek earth goddess) encouraged individuals to live in accordance with their natural surroundings. This is why the ancient Chinese developed *feng shui* and the architects of ancient Greece, and other cultures, innately appreciated that health, abundance and wellbeing relied on building homes, temples, palaces and theatres in keeping with the patterns found in nature.

For millennia the greatest thinkers, including Plato and

Pythagoras, have sought to understand the language of nature – indeed, life itself – through mathematics, particularly geometrical figures. Although traditionally regarded as male-dominated subjects, both geometry and mathematics were depicted in the sixteenth-century work *Margarita philosophica* as female figures. Geometry is seen as embodying the kind of intuitive, creative, contemplative approach associated with the feminine principle, while mathematics since Pythagoras has been divided into even, feminine numbers and odd, masculine ones.

Sacred geometry, the paradoxical fusion of logic with mysticism, is a metaphor for universal existence, from which we discover the importance of the circle, spirals and curves. More importantly, it was through studying the measurements and relationships of natural forms and integrating these into daily life that it was believed that the mind – through the physical manifestation of the earth – could receive symbolic messages from the heavens. This intermediary role of the human mind between eternal, Divine consciousness and the realm of the experiential is represented geometrically by the Vesica Piscis – the intersection of two identical, overlapping circles. It is believed that human consciousness acts as a balance between the unchanging reality of universal consciousness and the fluctuating actuality of empirical consciousness. In order to do this, human consciousness must be comprised of both. We are in the Divine and the Divine is in us; there is no separating the two.

Why this Process Works

This is the principle, 'things that accord in tone vibrate together; things that have affinity in their innermost natures seek one another', which is the oldest principle in the universe.

Nguyen-Dang-Thuc

In the late nineteenth century, a US inventor and polymath

named John Ernst Worrell Keely postulated a concept which he termed sympathetic vibration. By harnessing this subtle natural force, hitherto ignored at least by orthodox thinkers, Keely is reputed to have operated a basic hand-held machine that was powerful enough to disintegrate a mine full of quartz and to have designed a motor that ran on water. Throughout his thirty years of work, Keely is said to have rediscovered forty natural or universal laws, all based on the principle that everything resonates and that energy in the form of vibratory waves precedes matter.

Keely was a contemporary of those physicists such as Einstein who were working in the then new field of subatomic physics known as quantum mechanics and who, through their greater understanding of the structure of the atom, helped change erroneous assumptions about the nature of the universe. According to a physicist of a much earlier generation, Sir Isaac Newton (1642–1727), the atom was like a billiard ball, hard and inpenetrable, with very distinct and separate boundaries. Quantum reality, on the other hand, postulates that atoms are not solid matter at all, but comprise multi-levelled fields of vibrating energy. We see or experience matter, light, heat, sound, colour or whatever as being different simply because they are vibrating at differing rates.

The analogy extends to relationships between people. It has been suggested that the reason why we are attracted to some individuals and repulsed by others is to do with matching frequencies and resonance. When a tuning fork tuned to the note A is sounded near a set of piano strings, all the strings tuned to that note will vibrate while the rest will not. Similarly, we experience a sympathetic vibration with those people whose personal subatomic resonance is in harmony with our own.

Keely took practical steps to apply what Einstein termed Unified Field Theory, which states that all matter is organised energy – a conclusion that would not have surprised our ancestors millennia earlier. For example, in many ancient Eastern philosophies – such as the Hindu scriptures known as the *Vedas*, written c.2500 BC – the cosmos was considered to be composed of condensed matter that emanated from universal energy. What John Keely did was to systematically articulate the laws governing the inter-action of etheric forces and matter so that man could 'work a wondrous change in his methods of manipulating matter'. Few at the time took Keely seriously and he was either ridiculed or ignored for his pains; his work subsequently became lost to all bar a small minority interested in conspiracy theories.

The reason why Keely's discoveries aren't more widely known is partly because they would be commercially explosive. After all, what would the big multinationals which profit from the exploitation of natural resources such as oil and gas do if the public knew about the concept of free energy and could tap into this source? A further explanation may be that, unshackled by the specialisation that limits orthodox scientists, Keely took a holistic approach to his discoveries. In line with all the greatest creative geniuses, his enquiring mind was comfortable embracing mathematics and metaphysics, philosophy and the physical sciences, geometry and God. But generalists are inevitably treated with scepticism, if not derision.

As we move into the twenty-first century, however, this holistic approach is gaining momentum among those at the forefront of scientific achievement, resulting in greater acceptance of an inherent interconnectedness throughout nature. This relationship prompted one expert in chaos theory to suggest that a butterfly fluttering its wings in the Amazon could cause a tidal wave in Japan.

But what has all this got to do with the eight-step process you are about to undertake? Simply that the labyrinthine journey involves changing the vibrational level of your thoughts to a more elevated state to enable you to access your Higher Self or Higher Mind, to achieve the higher state of consciousness from which all lasting change occurs.

Eminent polymaths who view the universe as a complex, cosmic web of infinite vibrational energy no longer regard it as a Newtonian machine but as a holographic mind. This is the mind of what many choose to call God – a Divine Intelligence of which we and everything that is manifest or unmanifest are a part. It is a single vibratory source and, if we could only learn to elevate our own minds to resonate at a similar level, we would have access to the universal mind or mind of God.

The fascinating thing about a holograph is that, when split, each of the parts contains everything that was within the original whole. This is one explanation for what Jung termed the collective unconscious and why mystics believe that, as individual parts of the holographic cosmic consciousness or mind of God, we each contain the knowledge of everything that has ever been, is, or ever will be. All the secrets of the universe are there for us to excavate; we just need to relearn how.

For thousands of years, our wisest forebears have taught that the way to attune our minds to vibrate at a more refined level and tap into the universal mind is through spiritual practice, involving introspection, meditation and mental focus. The Taoist sage Chuang Tzu put this elegantly when he said: 'Control the mind. Attain one-pointedness. Then the harmony of heaven will come down and dwell in you.' What you are encouraged to do within the labyrinth, and through the guided visualisations and exercises that form part of your journey, is to harmonise your thoughts at this heavenly rate, realising the destiny that has been assigned to you. And, because energy and matter are one and the same, when you 'change your mind' the environment has no option but to change also to support that new state.

Self-creating Reality

This chapter is called 'The Internal Lock' because, as I tell my coaching clients over and over again, the door to your new, more fulfilled life can only be unlocked from deep within yourself. Only then will your external environment change to reflect the new you. Since our thoughts create our reality, how could it be otherwise? This message is illustrated by a story I like to relate at my workshops about a wise old man sitting on a rock just outside a village. As newcomers arrive they are anxious to discover what kind of reception they are likely to get from their new neighbours. One day an aggressive-looking couple stop on their way to taking up residence in the village.

'What kind of people live here, then?' asked the husband gruffly, his wife scowling alongside.

'What kind of people lived in your last village?' challenged the old man.

'Real scoundrels,' answered the newcomer. 'That's why we decided to move – I've never been in such a company of miserable, unhelpful, whinging individuals.'

The wise old man shrugged and said, 'Then I have to tell you that you can expect something like that here, too.'

'I knew it,' grumbled the man to his wife. 'That's the way of the world.'

Some time later another couple walked by, their life-long possessions wrapped up in cloth.

'Please tell us,' smiled the woman, gently patting the old man on the arm. 'We're new to this area. What are the inhabitants of this village like to live among?'

The wise old man gratefully took the food and drink that the couple offered him before asking, 'What kind of people lived in your last village?'

Both travellers laughed and began to sing the praises of their kind, loving and supportive neighbours and how sorry they were to have to leave them.

> 'Well, I have good news for you,' the old man
> delighted in telling them. 'That's exactly what you
> will find people to be like here too.'

The good news for *you* is that accessing your Higher Self
offers enormous benefits, both in terms of how you see
yourself and how others treat you. This point was made
clear to Barbara, one of my coaching clients, as she strug-
gled with her family's scepticism over her ability to run her
own business.

CASE HISTORY: Barbara's Story

Barbara suffered – like most of us at one time or another –
from low self-esteem. But, having worked unhappily for a
number of unenlightened employers since leaving college,
she was passionate about setting up her own design
consultancy and believed this to be part of her life's
mission. She announced her intention to her family, particularly her two older brothers – both highly successful, prag-
matic lawyers whom she asked to invest in her business –
but was dismayed to find situations from her past being
thrown back at her. Her family reminded her of the debts
she had run up in her early twenties, of the fact that she
had chosen unsuitable boyfriends (her brothers cited this
as an example of her not being a good judge of character),
and that as an employee she had taken rather a lot of sick
leave.

As is frequently the case, her family – though loving
Barbara enormously and with only what they thought were
her best interests at heart – were operating on the basis of
the only information they had to work with. They were relating to how Barbara had been in the past, and not to how she
might be in the future. During one particular coaching
session Barbara told me of her frustration at not being able
to persuade her family that things would be different if only
she was allowed to express her passion. I suggested that she
should take a different approach. Instead of trying to change
everyone else, why not go into the labyrinth with the intention

of changing herself, particularly her self-esteem issues? After all, the responsibility for demonstrating what she *could be* rather than being shackled by what she *had been* lay with Barbara alone.

Over a couple of weeks Barbara worked intensively through the eight-step process outlined in this book, particularly valuing Pathway 4 which deals with changing your behaviour in order to change your thoughts about yourself. Having visualised a successful, thriving business in which the investment she needed was available (there was no need to state its source – Barbara agreed to 'detach' from that), she embarked on a series of actions, from working on a detailed business plan to discussing other practical elements of her new operation with a local Small Business Adviser, as exemplified by Pathways 2 and 6.

The strong intuition this young woman experienced while working through the exercises for Pathway 5 fired her up in such a way that no one who met her could have doubted her passion and future success as a freelance design consultant. By the time she reached Pathway 8 (Living Your Destiny), having learned to trust that the universe wanted her to be fulfilled and happy, Barbara was so acceptable to herself that she could not fail to be acceptable to others. Without argument or even much discussion, her brothers phoned her out of the blue to say how proud they were of their younger sister and how delighted they would be to invest in her new venture.

Because of the interconnectedness of all things and the fact that thought is just another form of universal energy, when Barbara began to think of herself in a more elevated, empowered way her brothers' thoughts were magically transformed in line with that new thinking. While it is still early days for Barbara's business, she keeps the financial side in order (with a little help from various sources), has learned to engage her heart and head when making decisions over staffing, and has never been happier or healthier.

Change your Attitude, Transform your Life

As Barbara's story highlights, it is how you think about yourself that most influences others and enhances your chances of success. This is something you can develop irrespective of your educational background, professional qualifications or experience. The importance of the right kind of attitude has often been underestimated, yet I passionately believe it is the most important indicator of success in today's world of work.

In a TV documentary about a group of young showbusiness wannabes trying to make it in New York, the directors who were auditioning them said that the one thing that indicated which ones would make it and which wouldn't was their attitude, rather than their acting, singing or dancing talents. In fact most of us are aware of countless examples in showbusiness whereby individuals who are low on talent manage to achieve success through having high levels of self-belief, motivation and drive.

There's nothing like self-confidence to boost career or relationship success. A strong belief in myself is what has underpinned my own working life. Opportunities have serendipitously opened up in journalism, broadcasting and now within the sphere of personal development, and instead of wondering whether I had the appropriate experience or paper qualifications I've simply gone with the flow and done the best job I could. Having a burning desire to live out your potential *and* make a difference in the world is the most impressive attribute on any job application – and both of them come from within.

Psychologist Dr Abraham Maslow said something similar when he pondered what it was that accounted for some people selling themselves short at work. Having once attributed career success to a special talent and hard work, Maslow added that 'plain nerve' was also a major factor. He cited the example of someone who acts in a nervy, arrogant and artistic way being accepted and treated by others as an artist. And psychologists and personal development trainers frequently suggest individuals take on the attributes of the person they wish to become so that even if it feels inauthentic at first, this new behaviour soon becomes second nature.

When you believe your life to have purpose and meaning, you automatically take the responsibility to look after yourself physically, mentally and emotionally. You become more accountable for what you put into your body – the food you eat, how much fresh, unpolluted water you drink, whether you should continue smoking and imbibing alcohol so regularly; this is discussed further in Chapter 7. Positive thoughts breed more positive thoughts, and in order to support this you may decide to weed out of your life anyone who might infect you with their aura of negativity. It becomes important to be only in the company of generous, loving, supportive individuals who energise and inspire you.

Again, this state is not dependent on your external circumstances, as the renowned psychiatrist Viktor E. Frankl illustrated in his moving account of life in the Nazi concentration camps of World War II, entitled *Man's Search for Meaning*. If you think that positive, self-nurturing and loving thoughts are only possible when your life is good, I urge you to read his book, apply Frankl's insights to your own life and decide whether to take the opportunity to make your life an 'inner triumph' or a 'provisional existence'.

Giving up the Illusion of Control

Using the analogy of a physical journey, let's examine where we are so far. You've discovered the theory, in the same way that you might read as much as you can about a country or place you were about to visit. But before you get out your map and pack your bags, as it were, there is one very necessary preparation for any challenging voyage that many people foolishly ignore: the need to be mentally prepared.

Control is a conceit. It's about being in competition with the Divine – surely the greatest arrogance any human being can display. Yet there are very strong, human reasons why we become rooted to an addiction which requires everything to turn out exactly how we want it to. After all, almost from the moment we are born we are immersed in a world still shackled by the Newtonian view that life adheres to a small number of predictable laws that allow human beings to control their environment. This attitude has influenced thinking in education and management as well as the sciences. But it negates any sense of a bigger picture or purpose to life, and certainly to what the ancients recognised to be the interconnected patterns of life.

As we discovered in Chapter 1, there are no absolutes, only probabilities. By trying to impose our expectations on a complex, chaotic and uncertain universe, we are setting ourselves up for failure and disappointment. Giving up the illusion of control is the first step towards living a life of supreme fulfilment. The next step is to break free from the Newtonian view of a mechanistic, purposeless, meaningless existence and accept that there is a dynamic grand design in which we have the potential to feel loved, cherished and fulfilled beyond our wildest dreams. This means trusting that everything is working out for our highest good, so that we no longer have to fear failure or believe we can't cope with success.

CASE HISTORY: Jill's Story

A self-confessed control freak, Jill got into a frenzy when things didn't adhere to her timetable. She held everyone to their word, and when prospective clients or even friends failed to get in touch exactly when they had said they would she let it throw her life into turmoil. She even alienated a number of business contacts by continually chasing them when, unknown to her, their decisions had been delayed because of the procrastination of third parties.

Finally, in a state of complete exhaustion bordering on depression, Jill asked me why life was so tough on her, why she had to fight for everything all the time and expend so much energy. I suggested that it wasn't 'life' that was cracking the whip, but Jill's ego in wanting to order events so precisely. Over a period of months Jill began practising 'letting go'. I urged her to put up a big sign bearing the words 'Everything unfolding as it should'. When meetings didn't go ahead as planned, she was to believe there was a good reason. When clients didn't get back to her immediately, she was to accept that there was probably something holding them up that Jill wasn't aware of. And when work didn't come in as expected, Jill was to understand that this created a space in her life for something better to come along.

This new approach wasn't easy for Jill but, not liking the toll on her mental and physical health caused by her previous attitude, she agreed to give it a try. On one occasion during our coaching sessions Jill was in tears of frustration about a major project that had fallen through at the last minute, leaving her with a severe shortage of income. When we talked about this she admitted that it was only the money which had tempted her – the work involved was both tedious and highly pressurised. Since Jill was obviously ignoring some of her core values and her vision only to take on work that creatively stimulated and excited her, she accepted that she wasn't being allowed to undermine herself in this way. A grand plan was gradually unfolding in her life, as it is in all our lives, and its details just hadn't been made known to her at this time.

Two months later Jill announced that she was leaving the UK to work in Seattle, having always harboured a desire to move to the US. Her name had been put forward out of the blue for an exciting new business venture, offering a huge increase in salary doing work she was passionate about. Had the original UK-based project gone ahead, Jill would have had to sign a two-year contract and would therefore have been unable to take up this golden opportunity.

Jill is now a changed woman. When I last spoke to her about a joint venture that had hit a dead end she was sanguine. These days, she said, her stress levels are considerably reduced because she's happy just to go with the flow of events rather than trying to swim upstream all the time.

Always remember: if you have no expectations you cannot be disappointed. Expectations are synonymous with the desire to control. Try to rid yourself of them whenever possible.

Giving up the Habit

Human beings are said to want two basic things: the first is to experience pleasure, and the second is to avoid pain. The wisdom of Eastern spiritual teachers such as Buddha, Confucius and Lao Tsu, the founder of Taoism, teaches us that pain and suffering are inextricably bound up with desire and expectation. As one of the Four Noble Truths in Buddhism articulates: freedom from attachment leads to freedom from suffering.

This section describes some of the subconscious pay-offs which are chaining you to the habits of self-sabotage and procrastination. If you can always justify not taking a positive form of action, it could be for one of the following reasons.

Firstly, maybe your goals are not compelling enough. You think you want something, but when push comes to shove you're just not sufficiently motivated to put in the effort required. Motivation is an area in which very little psychological study has been done. However, we do know that human beings are compelled to make changes in their lives for two major reasons: because they are drawn towards something positive or away from something negative, and sometimes both at the same time. Much depends on you as a unique individual and the specific situation you are in. For example, you may not have a clear idea of your ideal career, but decide to leave your job anyway because you cannot stand another day operating like a robot. Alternatively, you may be very clear about the kind of relationship you want but don't yet know how to attract the ideal partner into your life. Or you are compelled to do something about increasing your finances because you have a passion for travel or fear poverty.

Unlike standard coaching techniques, which require you to articulate consciously what you want from your life, the eight-step process and supplementary exercises in this book are designed to ensure that what you desire comes from your heart and not just from your head. This represents the deeper knowing of your Higher Self. That is why they work. All you are required to do is to contribute a level of motivation for changing your life.

Secondly, when you fail to achieve your dreams you are providing yourself with evidence to support your own or someone else's negative opinion of you. You've convinced yourself that, because of past experiences or because someone has drummed it into you at an early age, you can't do something. So by sabotaging your chances you get to prove yourself right. When this happens you need to get into the habit of looking for evidence of all the things you *have* achieved in your life, and to have a more positive internal dialogue.

That's why, in coaching, we ask people to outline their achievements in a particular area of their lives, and not just to highlight the obstacles they need to overcome and the development skills they need to accrue in order to move themselves closer to their goals. If you always come up with reasons not to risk moving into a new, more fulfilling area of work, try listing your personal assets and past achievements to demonstrate that you really do have a 'can do' attitude when you put your mind to it.

The third subconscious pay-off for failing to fulfil your

divine potential is that you get to justify your life. This results in the tendency to say, 'I could have been this, but . . .' and to make a mental list of all the reasons why you've never lived up to your fullest possibilities. This usually involves blame of one kind of another – that your parents didn't force you to stay on at school or go to university, the right training wasn't available in the area, your partner held you back, you chose to have kids and that made it difficult to realise your ambitions. . . . The list is endless. What this boils down to is abdicating responsibility for yourself. After all, there is no chance of failing if you don't *do* anything.

Life is neither good nor bad – it's simply about making choices. Do you want to get to the end of your life and say, 'If only . . .'? Or do you want to embark on the hero's journey with all its potential ups and downs, and learn to enjoy the ride as well as the destination?

The fourth and final reason why we tend to sabotage our chances of success and personal fulfilment is particularly relevant if you have a coach, mentor, parent, teacher or even boss who recognises your potential and is doing everything in their power to move you forward while you are stubbornly staying where you are. This represents the desire to dominate – to play subconsciously into the hands of those negative demons inside you which say, 'Look, they think they're so smart, but – let's face it! – people like you never get the breaks. Why not give up now before you become dispirited or bitter?'

By invalidating the help that other people are trying to give you, you are not only supporting that negative internal dialogue you have got into the habit of playing to yourself, but you're maintaining control of your situation. Your fear of failure – a protective shell you have drawn around yourself so as not to be hurt by life – wants to gain the upper hand, so you will thwart every attempt by others to push you beyond your comfort zone. This was true of Frank, an occasional client of mine whom I consider to be virtually uncoachable.

CASE HISTORY: Frank's Story

Frank tried to dominate me by insisting we had inconvenient, face-to-face sessions even though telephone coaching is highly effective and this is the way I work with the rest of my clients. But most dysfunctionally, Frank made it impossible for me to help him move forward with his life by not doing the tasks – the 'action' part of our contract – that we had agreed he would undertake before our next session. He also vehemently refused to enter the labyrinth with me as his guide because he said he didn't like all this 'touchy-feely stuff'. I suspect that something from his childhood or early adulthood experiences is causing this man to self-sabotage as a way of getting other people's attention. Because I am a coach and not a therapist this was something it was not appropriate for me to explore with him, and as far as I know Frank has not investigated this with anyone else. He just isn't ready to move forward with his life yet, and therefore 'playing' at being coached is a waste of our time and his money.

In any self-development process, the most important word is 'self.' Until a person recognises that he or she not only needs to but *wants* to undertake the personal journey into the labyrinth, there is nothing anyone else can do. However, just becoming aware of the ways in which you subconsciously sabotage your right to a fulfilling and personally satisfying life is the first step to changing things for the better. Journeying into the labyrinth takes that desire for change one stage further and is the means by which countless pilgrims across many centuries and cultures have achieved a oneness with the Divine. But it helps to be in the right frame of mind before you start. Take a moment, therefore, to perform the following exercise.

EXERCISE: Find your Fear

Which of the habits outlined earlier have, in the past, prevented you from living the life you truly want. Have you:

- not given enough time and thought to articulating compelling goals for yourself?
- bought into the belief that you don't deserve a happy, fulfilling life?
- bought into someone's else's belief that life can never be happy and fulfilling?
- a fear of failure?
- a fear of success?
- a desire to prove yourself right and everyone else wrong, even if that means engaging in self-sabotaging behaviour and
  attitudes like replaying old emotional wounds from your childhood?
- become resentful of the limitations of your health, finances, location, gender, age or ethnicity, and are you using these as an excuse for lack of action?
- been so focused on competing with others or improving your social standing that you have ignored what is important to you as a unique individual?

If you are aware of a dysfunctional habit that you possess other than those listed above, use that instead. Write the habit at the top of a page in your notebook or journal. Then answer each of the following six questions in whatever order seems most appropriate:

- 'Why would that be so bad?'
- 'Where did this belief come from?'
- 'Who suffers most from this attitude/behaviour?'
- 'What is the worst that can happen?'
- 'How realistic is that?'
- 'How can you demonstrate that your fear is unjustified?'

The idea is to answer the first of those questions in relation to what you have written at the top of the page. Once you have done that answer the next question, again in relation to the last thing you wrote. Continue until you have completed all six sets of questions, repeating any as appropriate.

Example:

The reason why I have not achieved the life I long for is because I am afraid of failing.

'Why would that be so bad?' Because I would not only look a fool but disappoint my partner/children/parents.
'Where did this belief come from?' My parents, since I was always expected to succeed in everything I did; failure was not an option.
'Who suffers most from this attitude/behaviour?' Me. I feel under such a lot of pressure all the time, which is why I have avoided doing anything with any degree of risk.
'What is the worst that can happen?' I give something my best shot, it doesn't work out – and everyone thinks I am a total failure.
'How realistic is that?' Well, things might not work out on that occasion but it's unlikely that I'm going to fail at everything I attempt – that's certainly not been the case in the past.
'How can you demonstrate that this fear is unjustified?' Just go ahead, do the best I can and see what happens.

In most cases, the end result of this exercise is something that challenges your mental impasse – taking some sort of action. Once you have accepted the need to face your fears and are prepared to work through them, it's time to take some final, preparatory steps towards finding the fulfilling life you deserve. This is what we are about to cover in Chapter 3. Follow me. . . .

3

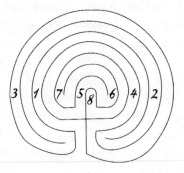

GETTING PREPARED

You must quiet the mind so the heart can hear,
because it is when the sacred enters your heart that
the mysteries begin to reveal themselves.

Phyllis Curott, contemporary Wiccan High Priestess, lawyer and author of
Book of Shadows

Before outlining the practical considerations you need to have in place before you can set out on your journey, let's just recap on what this will entail.

As explained in the Introduction, each of the eight steps of the labyrinth process involves focusing, through the technique of visualisation, on a specific subject. These are:

Pathway	
1	Vision
2	Tension
3	Detail
4	Change
5	Intuition
6	Diversity
7	The Unknown
8	Destiny

The benefits and technique of visualisation are described fully in Chapter 4. This chapter tells you how to create an audiotape of the various preparatory and labyrinth visualisations that are an essential feature of this eight-step process and expand on the topics listed above. You can either listen to your tape while in a relaxed state and visualise yourself walking through your imaginary labyrinth with eyes closed; or trace your finger along the pathways of a drawn labyrinth in order to induce a state of calm, as early worshippers did. For that, you will need to practise drawing labyrinths.

How to Draw your Labyrinth

The 'seed labyrinth' or basic form (see illustration on p. 66) comprises a cross into which are inserted four L-shapes with a dot in each corner. Once you have this basic form, drawing the Classical Seven-circuit Labyrinth is as easy as the 'join the dots' games we used to play as children.

- Place your pen or pencil at the top of the cross (see figure 1) and connect it with a curve to the next line end to create a hoop.

- Then, moving from the line end positioned directly to the left of the cross to the top right-hand corner dot, draw another curve (see figure 2).

- Continue this process, moving from the next left to the next right line endings or dots, always curving your lines as you do so (see figures 3–8).

- Don't worry if your efforts are a little wiggly at first. Drawing labyrinths perfectly – like riding a bicycle without having to concentrate too hard – takes practice. Take several large sheets of paper and, after drawing the basic form as shown in the illustration, continue with your labyrinth drawings until you have one that you feel happy to work with.

The Classical Seven Circuit Labyrinth

- You may wish to colour in the various pathways –
  either individually or in groups according to the
  principles of Dream, Do and Detach.

Tracing the Labyrinth with your Finger

Many people who have used the eight-step labyrinthine
process prefer to have their eyes closed while visualising
their journey, which makes it impossible to trace the pathways accurately. If you feel likewise, or if you have
impaired eyesight, buy some pipe cleaners or other bend-
able, stick-like material and, cutting and shaping the pieces

to fit, glue them over the drawn lines of your paper labyrinth. You can then easily follow the edges of the pipe cleaner to keep you on track as you trace along the various paths with your fingers. If you are artistic or inventive you may come up with other ways in which the 'walls' of your labyrinth can be raised slightly to make sure your finger stays on track when your eyes are closed.

Enhancing the Labyrinth

If there are any other enhancements you wish to make to your labyrinth, go ahead. Make the final version as big as you like, beautifully coloured and maybe even with curved loops or lunations, such as are found on the Chartres labyrinth, on the perimeter (see illustration on p. 37). As long as your labyrinth has seven pathways and a centre, no matter how you embellish it, you will still have the perfect tool with which to undertake the eight-step process.

Altered States: Deep Relaxation

Most self-help books suggest that you visualise the future you feel most compelled to achieve for yourself as a first step towards finding greater happiness and fulfilment in your life. This is not the same as just thinking about what you want. As explained earlier, one of the challenges I face as a life coach is to help my clients excavate what their hearts and souls are trying to tell them, not just their heads. When you operate at a conscious level you often limit yourself with the attitudes, beliefs and assumptions that shackle your spirit.

It is important, therefore, to induce in yourself an altered state of consciousness before entering, and while tracing/walking, the labyrinth. One of the ways to do this without resorting to mind-altering drugs is through deep relaxation. When deeply relaxed, the mind and body can accomplish amazing things. For example, through a relaxation technique known as biofeedback it is possible to train yourself consciously to alter your heartbeat, rate of blood flow, brainwaves and many other physiological processes that are generally considered to be out of our control. Yoga induces a similar state through which the stressors of modern living can be curbed. Chapter 4 details some of the achievements of artists and scientists during various self-induced states of relaxation.

There are two main components of deep relaxation or meditation. The first relates to the breath: focusing on your breath is an essential part of accessing your Higher Self. In many cultures the words for breath and spirit are synonymous or very similar, as with the Hebrew term *ruach*, the Greek *pneuma* and the Latin *spiro*. Practise concentrating on slowing down your breathing and notice how, as you do so, your focus shifts away from the chattering of your thoughts. I like to describe the creative and other insights offered by the Higher Self as being like a whisper which cannot ordinarily be heard until the cacophony produced by the conscious mind is quietened. As you undergo the various guided visualisations that are part of this labyrinthine journey, the way you breathe is a necessary element in the process.

Daily Stressbuster

As a daily stressbuster, every so often stop what you are doing and take three deep, slow breaths, allowing your body to relax as you exhale. Buddhist mystic and teacher Thich Nhat Hanh suggests that as you do so you think to yourself:

> *Breathing in I smile*
> *Breathing out I relax*
> *This is a wonderful moment.*

EXERCISE: The Cleansing Breath

As a longer, more empowering exercise, build in some time every day to concentrate on the process of breathing. Find a quiet, comfortable place where you can sit undisturbed for at least ten minutes. Turn your attention to the life-giving experience of breathing, a process we take for granted yet which is so vital for present-moment awareness. As you breathe in and out, focus on the feeling of the air through your nostrils. Keep your full attention on that area of your body for a while, ensuring that each exhalation completely expels all the air you breathed in. This not only helps your body expel more toxic waste but ensures that your lungs are emptied and can take in more new air.

Now change your focus to the way your abdomen rises and falls. Become aware of how much of your lungs are expanding with each in-breath. If you have become a habitual shallow breather, as many of us have, you are not making use of their full capacity. Place a hand on your stomach. If it rises as you breathe in and sinks as you exhale then you are breathing properly, extending the abdomen. If, instead, your shoulders rise and fall as you breathe, mentally practise pushing each breath of fresh air into the deeper reaches of your lungs before expelling it fully.

As you breathe in this way, become aware of how challenging you find it to control your mind's desire to pull you away and shift your attention to fantasies, past, present and future.

Witnessing your Thoughts

The next component of deep relaxation is called witnessing your thoughts. The Ego is like a demanding child, always looking to grab your attention when you have deeper, more meaningful things you could be attending to. While you attend to its superficial focus you are missing out on the wisdom of that whispering other, your Higher Self.

Again, try to spend some time every day taking an objective perspective on your thoughts, particularly negative and disempowering ones. Imagine that you are not connected to your thoughts but have been asked to be an impartial witness to them. When you objectively view your thoughts in this way and choose not to manipulate them, you will soon realise that you are not your thoughts and that you always have a choice of what you focus on in life – a concept that will be further explored in Chapter 7. For the moment, remember the words of Buddha:

> *We are what we think.*
> *All that we are arises with our thoughts.*
> *With our thoughts we make the world . . .*
> *The task is to quieten them,*
> *And by ruling them to find happiness.*

EXERCISE: Present-moment Awareness

Consciously controlling your thoughts requires present-moment awareness. Here's another exercise to help you to develop this life-enhancing state.

Begin to train your mind to be less frantic by attending to just one thing at a time. Start by doing this for, say, ten minutes a day. If you are washing dishes, focus on the feel of the water on your hands, the texture of the plates, the steely hardness of the cutlery. Look at what you are doing rather than gazing out of a window or thinking about what you have to do next. Don't have anything else going on in the background; turn off the TV or radio and learn to be comfortable with the silence.

If you are sweeping the back yard, in the words of Martin Luther King Jnr: 'Sweep . . . even as Michelangelo painted or Beethoven composed music, or Shakespeare wrote poetry. . . '. Really pay attention to whatever it is you are doing, the person you are with or the food you are eating. Suddenly, the most mundane of activities will take on new meaning: life will become richer and more enjoyable if you rediscover the joys contained in even the simplest of tasks. Yes, it can seem insignificant or tedious to clean your home, keep the windows sparkling and polish the floors. But if you regard maintaining a beautiful environment as one of the ways in which you honour yourself, you will recognise that an element of the Sacred is contained in even the most ordinary of tasks. Develop this principle of present-moment awareness – after all, it's the only reality we have – for longer and longer each day, and see it for the gift it is.

Close Encounters of the Universal Kind

Why does deep mental and physical relaxation bring about so many life-enhancing benefits? Because when you combine the conscious and the subconscious in this way you get access to the superconscious or subliminal mind. It is this state that was once regarded as aiding people to indulge in sorcery and magic – a word, incidentally, that is closely associated with *magus*, the name given to the three wise men who brought gifts to the infant Christ, and hence implies wisdom. When you are totally relaxed both mentally and physically, this 'letting go' of conscious control allows you to become imbued with universal wisdom.

Physicist and philosopher Danah Zohar offers a quantum theory explanation of how the deeper insights and creative potential associated with this 'letting go' often result in precognition – knowing something we did not know we knew or did not believe it is possible to know. In her book *Through the Time Barrier: A Study of Precognition and Modern Physics*, Zohar explains how, when in a reduced state of activity such as during meditation, a greater proportion of the neurones in the brain are susceptible to 'stimulation by quantum indeterminate phenomena'. In other words, we are in the right state to 'tune in' to quantum reality and access the vast cosmic web of interconnected potential that is the universe. As an analogy, imagine that, instead of only being able to access the contents of one book, through deep relaxation you would be able to download into your brain every bit of information in every library that has ever been built. Think of the potential that would open up for you!

Other Factors to Bear in Mind Before you Begin your Visualisation/Meditations

- If you choose to keep your eyes open in order to trace your paper labyrinth (without any enhancements) with your finger, focus totally on the illustration so that you will not become mentally distracted by other visual stimuli. The best way to do this is to half-close your eyes and keep them in soft focus – that is, to let your gaze rest gently on the labyrinthine diagram. Perhaps place your illustration on an unpatterned cloth or sheet in a shade that is restful to the eyes, like pale green or blue. Practise the most relaxing way to gaze at your labyrinth before undertaking the visualisation itself.

- Choose your environment with care: it should be peaceful, quiet, private, warm, well-ventilated and comfortable. Light scented candles or burn fragrant incense sticks if you feel inclined to do so. If the phone rings or someone comes to the door, make sure you will not be disturbed.

- Choose your time with equal care. This journey cannot be rushed, so only embark on it when you have no pressing engagements that will play on your mind. Put a 'Do Not Disturb' sign on the door if appropriate. Try to be in the right frame of mind – neither too 'down in the dumps' nor euphoric. Pick times to enter the labyrinth when you are feeling emotionally balanced yet enthusiastic about this adventure, and remember to do the preparatory 'extraneous baggage' visualisation (see p. 74) to help you shake off any negativity.

- If you decide to play background music, will this enhance rather than detract from your experience? The most suitable sounds are those that have no lyrics – relaxing sounds from nature such as dolphin or whale songs or the trickle of water. But you may get clearer messages from just listening to the voice on your tape, with no extraneous noise to contend with.

- Have something to eat so that you won't be feeling hungry and therefore be distracted during your journey, but not so much that you feel bloated and uncomfortable. Wear loose clothing while undertaking the guided visualisations. Go to the toilet/bathroom just before you begin the labyrinth exercise so that a need to go won't distract you either.

- Look critically at the labyrinth you have drawn to use with this exercise. Is it big enough? Do you feel compelled by it? Whenever people have to work with unattractive 'tools' the whole experience is affected – don't let this be a problem for you. If you feel your drawing abilities are inadequate, do you know someone more skilled who could produce a large, attractive labyrinth for you?

Creating the Visualisation Audiotapes

1. Choose someone with a soothing, gentle voice to make this recording for you.
2. The occasional stumble or hesitation is natural in people who don't have training in recording audiotapes. Ask your volunteer to practise reading the copy several times before you make the final recording. If, while this is taking place, they make a mistake, only stop and re-record that section if you feel it would distract you during the visualisation itself.
3. While doing an initial run-through, make any necessary changes to the copy. For example, you may decide to change the occasional word so that it sounds more natural for the reader – but don't make wholesale changes to the content. Also cross out any words that don't apply, as in 'chair/bed/place on the floor and sit/lie down again'. Any words in brackets in the visualisation text are for guidance only and need not be recorded.
4. Once you and your 'voice-over' are happy, record your friend reading each of the following three guided visual-

isations in turn on one or more blank audiotapes. Make sure they take their time over this. The dots (. . .) at the end of each sentence indicate a gap. This needs to be long enough for you to have time to think about what it is you have just envisioned and experienced, but not so long that your mind begins to wander. You will need to tell your friend how long a gap they should leave.

5. Leave space on the tape between each of the three guided visualisations. Or you may wish to record them separately on to three audiotapes.

6. It may seem obvious, but do remember to label your audiotapes.

7. Have a glass of water or light snack available to help ground yourself at the end of each guided visualisation.

PREPARATORY RELAXATION
EXERCISE: Offloading Extra 'Baggage'

This will help you to achieve the most beneficial, relaxed state in which to begin the eight-step labyrinth process itself. It focuses on offloading unnecessary psychological and emotional baggage that can act as a barrier to receiving messages from your Higher Self.

Close your eyes. . . . Uncross your legs. Place both feet on the floor and rest your hands gently in your lap. Let your shoulders relax and get yourself into a comfortable position. . . . Now take a deep breath, hunch up all your muscles for a few seconds and, as you release them, let out a big sigh. . . . Do that three more times – breathe deeply, hunch up those muscles and sigh out all that pent-up tension . . . breathe . . . tighten your muscles from the top of your head to your toes. . . . And sigh. . . . Last time. Take a deep breath . . . tighten all the muscles in your body . . . and let out one big, final sighhhh. . . .

Now jiggle yourself about until you are in a position you can hold comfortably for the duration of this exercise. . . . Remember to keep your breathing slow and steady . . . slow and steady. . . .

Today you are going on a journey of creativity. . . . As with any journey, the lighter your load, the more comfortable and enjoyable it will be. . . . I now invite you to offload some of the emotional baggage you carry with you that could prevent you from getting the most out of this experience. . . . This baggage isn't required at this time, but you may still want to acknowledge its usefulness to you at other times. Be assured, therefore, that you can collect it at the end of this exercise and take it back – or not, as you wish. . . .

Imagine that you have a large bag or suitcase by the side of your chair. . . . You may or may not 'see' your suitcase in your mind's eye – you may be aware of it in other ways. . . . It doesn't matter whether you get a visual image or not, just let your imagination sense a large suitcase. . . . Now think a little more clearly about what your suitcase is like. What colour and shape is it? . . . Does it have a smell like leather or plastic? . . . How does it feel to hold the handle? . . . Are the edges smooth or rough? . . . Just how big is this bag or suitcase of yours? . . .

Now I invite you to reach down, in your mind's eye, and open up your suitcase. And to put into it all the emotional baggage which you will not need during the day. . . . Imagine all of these things as something visual – maybe a little animal, a shape or colour, a feeling or simply an undefined sense. . . . This represents your preconceived ideas and expectations about your journey into the labyrinth . . . what you do or do not want to get out of this expedition to find total fulfilment in your life . . . any concerns or worries you may have about working with your Higher Self . . . any fears about involving yourself in the exercises . . . put into your suitcase any shyness you may be feeling, any reluctance to 'join in' . . . any inhibitions. . . . Also, all your thoughts about what you are planning to do this evening, what's going on at home, or at work . . . what's going on in the world outside this room. . . . Pop into your suitcase all your cares, worries and concerns . . . thoughts about anyone other than yourself. . . . Place in your suitcase anything that may prevent you from giving and receiving 100 per cent fun, enjoyment and commitment to the eight-step process.

Now take a moment to think about anything else you would like to place in your suitcase that you don't need for the moment. Take your time over this. Remember to breathe slowly and deeply, relaxing your body and your mind.

(Pause for thirty seconds.)

Now I invite you to close your suitcase securely. Fix the clasp, lock it if necessary, and imagine yourself lifting it . . . how heavy it feels . . . and walking towards the door of this room. Now you are walking out of the door. . . . down the stairs (if applicable) . . . and out of the front door. . . . There, someone greets you whose job it is to look after this luggage. . . . He or she agrees to look after your bag or suitcase for you and gives you a ticket which you now take and place in your pocket. . . . Know that your suitcase will be securely locked away and can be collected by you at the end of this tape . . . if you want it back. Feel how light you are without that suitcase weighing you down. Light and free, energised and looking forward to fully participating in your journey into the labyrinth. Knowing that you are in a safe environment with Divine Goodness watching over you, about to embark on an exciting adventure that will herald a fresh approach to your life.

Now imagine yourself retracing your steps back to this room.. . . Up the stairs . . . along the hall . . . through the door until you are back in this room and have reached your chair/bed/place on the floor and sit/lie down again.

Take another few deep breaths and in your own time stretch your arms and legs, wiggle them about, get up if you feel like it and shake your body, then open your eyes. Welcome back. Now please take a drink of water or eat a light snack to ground yourself fully.

EXERCISE: Visualising your Personal Labyrinth

In the same way that it's a good idea to have a taster of unknown territory before embarking on a full-scale expedition, this guided visualisation works towards firmly establishing your personal labyrinth in your mind's eye. This is important, whether you do the journey by tracing your finger along the labyrinth with your eyes open or with your eyes closed. It is an opportunity to sense your labyrinth fully, and can be done once or several times before undertaking the eight-step process itself. The more clearly you can sense your labyrinth, the more realistic the experience will be for you. This enhances your results by confusing your conscious self into making the labyrinth a sensory experience and not just an intellectual exercise. After all, the mind cannot tell the difference between what is real and what is realistically imagined.

I would like you to close your eyes. Place both feet firmly on the floor with your hands resting gently in your lap. . . . Breathe in deeply and slowly. Once again, take a deep, slow breath and then tense all the muscles in your body. . . . Now release – letting out any sounds you need to express. Tense again and release. With each release you are becoming more and more relaxed . . . your mind calm . . . your emotions balanced. . . . Once more, tense and release. . . .

This is a journey into the imagination. You are about to create, in your mind's eye, your personal labyrinth, the one in which you will shortly begin your quest to rediscover your Higher Self . . . your life mission . . . the total fulfilment which you have been seeking and which comes from direct access to Divine Guidance. . . . In front of you is the entrance to a cave. But this is no ordinary cave. It is a labyrinth – a magical, mystical place, the symbol of your deep subconscious, the well from which spring all your creative thoughts. . . .

Take several steps forwards so that you are now just

inside your labyrinth. . . . Touch the wall to your right. . . .
How does it feel? . . . Is it warm or cold? . . . Dry or damp?
. . . Rough or smooth? . . . Get a sense of what being in
your labyrinth is like. . . . What colour is it? . . . Is it made
of one type of stone or several? . . . Is it made of stone at
all, or perhaps some other material? . . . Run your finger
along the wall and then place the finger in your mouth. . . .
What can you taste? . . . Something earthy, salty, or is there
no flavour at all?

What about the air? . . . If the temperature is too extreme
for you, you can adjust it at any time just by thinking of the
ideal state . . . make sure your body feels comfortable as you
move further and further into the labyrinth. . . .

Note the pleasant fragrance which permeates this place
as you walk along the corridor. . . . What is that smell? . . .
What does it remind you of? . . . Is it a comforting, warm-
ing smell like pine cones, cinnamon bark or dried rose
petals? . . . Is it fresh and energising like citrus fruits? . . .
Is it sweet and appealing like the smell of honey or vanilla?
. . . Or maybe there is no smell at all except that of cool,
fresh air. . . .

If at any time unpleasant thoughts come into your head
that affect your labyrinth, you have the power to change
them. This is your special place and you can reframe these
senses in any way you wish so that the labyrinth you will use
for the eight-step process is exactly the way you want it to be.

Now you are about to enter the labyrinth proper. Turn
to your left and sense the beginning of a long, winding
pathway. The pathway curves round slightly to the right
and slopes gradually downwards into the earth. . . . Follow
that pathway and, as you do, consider the floor beneath
you. Is it rough or smooth? . . . Is it made of cobblestones
or earth? . . . Or something completely different?
. . . Is the floor damp or dry? . . . Sense the texture as you
place one foot in front of another. . . .

What sounds do you hear? The crunching sound of gravel
underfoot, or the clear clip-clop of paving slabs? . . . In your

imagination, call out your name. . . . Is there an echo in the labyrinth?. . . What other noises are you aware of as you follow this curved pathway around to the right? . . .

Look above you. . . . Carved into niches in the labyrinth wall are candles to guide your way. . . . The light they throw out is soft and comforting. . . .

There is only you here and you are at ease with your own company. The pathways of the labyrinth are wide and welcoming, the air is warm and it is easy to breathe deeply. The silence is a relief from all the hurly-burly of life outside. It is so quiet you can hear your own heartbeat, the deepness of your breath and the steadiness of your footsteps. This is a special place, somewhere you can feel safe and secure and at home with your own thoughts.

Now I invite you to quicken your pace as you walk through the labyrinth. . . . The sloping walkway makes this effortless. You sense you are almost at the end of the first pathway. You come to what seems like a dead end. . . . But, as you draw near to the wall in front of you, you discover that there is a turning to the left and the pathway doubles back on itself on the other side. This is as far as you need to go for now. Simply turn round to retrace your steps along the first pathway to reach the mouth of the labyrinth. . . . As you walk along, assess your labyrinth. . . . Is it everything you had hoped it would be? . . . If not, make the changes now, as you are returning from this short journey . . . or make a mental note to alter them the next time you take this preparatory journey.

(Pause for ten seconds.)

The wall to your right is now curving gently inwards and the path has a gradual incline. . . . Up ahead you see a wall with a stream of light shining in from the right. . . . You have reached the entrance to the labyrinth again. . . . As you approach the wall in front of you, take a sharp turn to the right and leave the labyrinth. . . .

Now take a moment to fix, in your mind's eye, exactly what it looks, feels, smells, tastes and sounds like. . . .

(Pause for twenty seconds.)

Take a deep, slow breath and, as you open your eyes, stretch your arms and legs . . . take a sip of water to ground yourself . . . wiggle your fingers and toes . . . and when you feel ready, get up and walk about.

The Eight-step Labyrinthine Process for Finding Fulfilment

This visualisation is printed in full on p. 169. The relevant sections for each of the Dream, Do and Detach pathways are also given at the beginning of the next three chapters. However, it is important not to undertake any of the exercises in Chapters 4–7 until you have completed this imaginary journey.

The Rules of the Game

The labyrinth journey you are going to undertake is rather like a virtual reality game. There are few rules, and they are simple ones.

1. As you make your way through each pathway you will be encouraged to take part in a visualisation and/or think about some specific questions. Please take your time focusing on whatever insights come to you. If you think you might not remember them, make a few notes in your journal to work on later.

2. If at any time you are unhappy with the way your labyrinth looks or feels, you can reframe it to something more appropriate. The purpose of the preparatory labyrinth visualisation is to ensure you will be walking through a labyrinth in which you are happy and comfortable. This is the beauty of your imagination; while in everyday life you may suffer from claustrophobia, for example, your labyrinth can have pathways as wide and ceilings as high as you like. If you have a fear of the dark, your labyrinth can be beautifully lit with candles or splendid chandeliers. This personal labyrinth

is the product of your own dreams and desires – the only restrictions are those you place on yourself.

3. Please complete the labyrinthine journey in one session, if at all possible. Sometimes it may feel appropriate for you only to venture so far into your labyrinth – say, the first three pathways – and then retrace your steps and work on the symbolic messages offered to you from these Dream pathways. If you really feel it is important to accomplish your journey in stages, then go with your intuition. However, try to be sure that this is a message from your Higher Self and not from your ego. Remember, the ego does not want you to confront what may be unpalatable truths about your current life or which require you to fulfil the challenges presented by your Higher Self. It much prefers the status quo where it is comfortable. As a spiritual warrior, a hero, you are urged to accomplish the whole of the labyrinthine journey in order to break out of your confining comfort zone.

From End to Beginning

When you have undertaken all three visualisations and have completed your venture in the labyrinth, don't think your journey is over – it's just about to begin. The next three chapters outline, pathway by pathway, exercises that will help you develop the insights you have collected during the eight-step labyrinth process in order to find fulfilment in your life.

As with any form of symbolism, it would be impossible for me as your guide to state exactly what the personal insight gained from pathway eight means in the context of your own individual life. However, to help you interpret the symbolic messages offered to those whom I have accompanied through the labyrinth, Chapter 7 contains a number of case histories to show how various clients' journeys have resulted in their finding fulfilment in life in the context of work, personal relationships and finances.

Are you ready? It's time to go. . . .

4

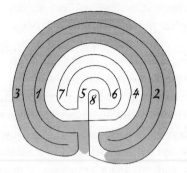

THE DREAM PATHWAYS

The slumber of the body seems to be but the waking of the soul.

Sir Thomas Browne, seventeenth-century English physican and writer

The Labyrinth Visualisation *Part 1*

Close your eyes. Make sure you are in a relaxed position, and that any stray thoughts entering your head that are not relevant to the labyrinthine process are acknowledged but allowed to float by like a fish in a stream. You cannot ignore the fact that the fish is there, but you can choose how much you focus on it. Remember, your focus is on the journey you are about to take . . . an exciting adventure into the depths of your being . . . the culmination of which will be accessing your Divine Potential and finding the fulfilment that you deserve in your life. Remember to breathe evenly and deeply, relaxing your body more and more with every breath you take . . . breathing out all tension and physical aches and pains with every exhalation.

You are standing at the mouth of your labyrinth. . . . You are light and free with only the clothes on your body and bare feet that connect you to the ground. . . . Take four steps forward so that you are surrounded on three sides –

*left, right and in front – by the walls of your labyrinth.
Take a moment to bring to mind what your labyrinth is
like. . . . Is the temperature warm or cool? . . . Are the walls
damp or dry? . . . What decoration, if any, is on them? . . .
Look down, in your mind's eye, at the floor. . . . What is it
made of? . . . What does it feel like? . . . Smooth or rough?
. . . Wet or dry? . . . What colour are the floor, the walls,
the ceiling? . . . Is there a fragrance in your labyrinth? . . .
If so, silently put a name to it. . . . Begin to walk ahead a
little until you reach the wall in front of you. . . . What
sounds do your footsteps make? . . . Is there an echo in
your labyrinth? . . .*

*Now turn to your left and begin walking into Pathway 1
. . . it is illuminated, making your labyrinth a safe, comfortable, exciting place to be for you at this time. . . .*

*As you walk along this, the first of the Dream pathways,
become aware that the wall to your right is covered with a
screen. On the floor by your feet is a remote control handset. Press the big red button on the handset now. This
allows you to watch your current life projected five, ten,
fifteen years or more from now. . . . This story is the result
of the present course you have set your life on . . . the result
of the current choices you are making. . . . You are watching where your relationship with your partner is heading
. . . your career path . . . the people who are in your life
including children . . . members of your extended family . . .
and friends. . . . You are aware of your future health . . .
your financial situation . . . where you are living. . . . At any
time you can press the pause button to concentrate on any
particular scene. . . .*

(Pause for ten seconds.)

*As you watch this future life, the extension of the life
path you are currently on . . . be aware of any discomfort
in your mind or body related to any of these areas. . . . You
have the power to change your future in any way you
desire. . . . That power is in your hands right now. . . . Be
aware that you can fade out any part of this future that you*

do not wish to happen.... And, by pressing another button on your handset marked 'New Future', you can change that scene to whatever is most desirable to you and in keeping with the wisdom of your Higher Self.... Do this now....

(Pause for twenty seconds.)

Now it's time to turn round another bend into the next pathway ... the pathway of tension.... The walls of this second pathway curve gently from right to left.... Take a deep breath.... Smell the fragrant, fresh air.... Feel the floor beneath your feet.... Be aware of your labyrinth through your all senses....

Be aware that you have come to an invisible, flexible force field.... This represents your comfort zone.... Think again about all the ways in which you wish your vision of the future to be different from the projection of the current path you viewed on the screen in Pathway 1. ... How do you wish it to be the same? ... Just be aware of any feeling of tension between where you are now and where you want to be ... the discomfort you feel about the way your current life is progressing.... Whether you are motivated away from the past and the present or towards the future doesn't matter.... You are fired up by the desire to change certain aspects of your life so that they become different from the current course it is on.

Hold that feeling as you push against the force field ... your comfort zone.... How resistant is it? ... Become aware of some of the specific differences between the life you have and the life you want.... The future you deserve is magnetic and compelling.... You are breaking through that force field ... now ... on to a new, more empowering and fulfilling course....

(Pause for ten seconds.)

You are entering Pathway 3, which covers the entire perimeter of your labyrinth ... there is no need to rush ... Take time to consider some of the changes you need to make in order to bring your ideal life, a life of total fulfilment, into your current reality....

Think about where you are now and what you need to commit yourself to doing to steer yourself firmly through the new course you have chosen. . . . What new attitudes, beliefs, behaviours and values do you now have to embrace to bring that about? . . . Briefly jot down any ideas that come to you. . . .

(Pause.)

Now imagine these new attitudes, beliefs, behaviours and values and this fresh sense of purpose, as a cloak lying on the floor of your labyrinth. . . . When you are ready, put it on . . . and move ever closer to your new destiny. . . .

Perchance to Dream. . . .

> *Vision is the art of seeing things invisible.*
> Jonathan Swift (1667–1745), Irish writer and satirist

Dreams have figured largely in the history of humankind. Yet despite recent scientific discoveries about how the brain works, no one has been able to come up with a conclusive explanation for why we dream. Throughout history dreams and visions have frequently been portrayed as the means by which individuals have received insights about their destinies. It was the dreams of Joseph in the Old Testament which offered a premonition of his later greatness. On account of his ability to interpret the Pharaoh's dreams of fat cattle and grain being swallowed up by their gaunt and blighted counterparts, he was put in charge of building up the reserves which enabled Egypt to cope with the impending years of famine.

For Aboriginal Australians, Dreamtime was a time when their ancestral spirits created and lived on the earth and shapeshifted into various forms from animals to rocks. Today, Aborigines believe that those born close to Dreaming sites are the incarnations of the spirits connected with that place and therefore have a responsibility to look after it. For shamans (tribal medicine men) dreaming is also associated with the soul – demonstrating that it can leave the body each night and return without causing the dreamer to die.

Dreams and visions have also inspired some of the greatest works of art and music, inventions and scientific discoveries – and not always when the dreamer was unconscious. Einstein is said to have postulated his Theory of Relativity while daydreaming that he was riding the universe on a sunbeam. The German chemist Kekulé realised that the benzene molecule had a circular structure as he gazed into a fire and imagined he saw a flame like a snake, curling round and eating its tail. And composers Tartini, Wagner and even Paul McCartney are said to have 'heard' music in their dreams which they then wrote down upon waking.

A key factor in creative imaging is to imbue the images with a high emotional charge: you have to be passionate about what you are creating and be in an environment conducive to imaginary musings. However, in keeping with the universal laws outlined in this book, the results are most effective when you:

- undertake regular creative imaging (dream)
- act on the hunches or intuitive flashes that come to you (do), but
- don't become too anxious or consciously force them to work (detach)

Simply trust that this innate creative mechanism continues below your conscious awareness. Let the universe take care of the details!

The imagination is also a vital link to understanding and realising your divine purpose. The Irish writer George Bernard Shaw articulated this perfectly in his play *St Joan*, through an exchange between Joan of Arc and a military squire called Captain Robert de Baudricourt. She explains to the soldier that she hears voices telling her what to do and that they come from God. A sceptical de Baudricourt counters that surely they come just from her imagination, to which Joan replies: 'Of course. That is how the messages of God come to us.' Similarly, the Jewish *Torah* says: 'I the Lord make myself known to them in visions. I speak to them in dreams.'

Never think of your imagination – of the voices or images you receive in your mind – as being of no consequence. Like Joan, I believe they contain Divine messages when they come to you in the silent moments when your conscious mind and ego have dropped their guard. According to the late Mother Teresa: 'It is in the silence of the heart that God speaks.'

The problem is that, because we have ignored the Higher Self for so long, the frequency on which it transmits has grown fuzzy. Western minds are like a radio that hears several stations at a time because we don't take the time to tune into any of them properly. We are mainly focused on the day-to-day trivia poured out of the commercial stations, only hearing sporadically and imperfectly 'Divine FM'. When we take time to daydream, to keep a dream journal, to act on the creative hunches that nudge us towards greatness and to meditate, we are metaphorically tweaking the dial that offers a direct channel to God or the universal mind, and hence discover how to fulfil our unique potential.

Dream Exercise 1: Your Futurelife Chart

Buy a roll of lining paper or use the plain side of a sheet of non-adhesive wallpaper at least 10 feet long. Unfurl it from top to bottom so you have a long, tall strip of paper before you. Now draw a vertical line dividing the length equally into two, then horizontal lines across the roll 1 foot apart so that you have twenty 'boxes' in total. Now turn the paper through 90 degrees so that you have it widthways in front of you.

Along the left-hand edge of the paper, mark the upper box 'Positives – Non-changeable' and the box underneath it 'Negatives – Changeable'. Along the top of the paper give each of the other nine double sections a heading, according to the various important areas in your life. Your list might look like this:

1. Work/career
2. Partnership
3. Family and other close relationships
4. Social life
5. Health
6. Personal finances
7. Spiritual development
8. Fun
9. Community service

Other choices might be: Creative expression/hobbies; Travel; Further education; Personal development; Home environment. Just choose whatever aspects of life are of particular importance to you. If you want more than nine life areas on your chart, simply draw more sections.

Now recall the screenplay you watched on the wall of Pathway 1 as well as the insights about the new future you want to create from Pathway 2, and start filling in the appropriate boxes with what you visualised. If you viewed your health as being good well into the future, because you know how well you look after your mind and body today, write the details above the central line. If, however, the future did not look so rosy for your health and you want to change that, fill in the details below the central line. Be as explicit as you can, particularly about which aspects of each life area you construe as negative and therefore want to change. The two case histories here are good examples.

CASE HISTORY: Jane's Story

Looking into her projected future on Pathway 1, Jane had visualised an extremely soulless existence at work. One of the insights she gained on Pathway 2 was that it wasn't the nature of her work as a TV researcher that was the problem but the inhumane and spiritually bankrupt organisation she worked for. Jane visualised herself changing *where* she worked, but not her chosen career.

CASE HISTORY: Andy's Story

Andy, on the other hand, had visualised a future life with his partner in which the communication gap between them had grown to an unbridgeable chasm and he was unable to see any positive future with this person. After filling in the future-life chart, he recognised that their early relationship had been based purely on sexual attraction and, now that that had waned, their personal values and life goals were too disparate to sustain the relationship. Andy then had to consider whether to end the relationship; to stick it out and allow it to limp towards a barren future; or to communicate on a deeper level with his partner to search for more common ground. After trying the last of these choices he ultimately came to the conclusion that it was better for both of them if the relationship ended. Andy still uses the wisdom he gained from this part of the labyrinth process to discuss major life issues with prospective partners. This enables him to call a halt before becoming too emotionally involved with any woman who might lead him off track from his gloriously envisioned future.

Keep your futurelife chart somewhere safe as you will be using it alongside future exercises.

Tensed and Tensibility

> *Most of the time when we are blocked in an area of our life, it's because we feel safer that way.*
>
> Julia Cameron, author *The Artist's Way*

Let's make no bones about it: if you want your future life to be different, something has to change *now*. And that inevitably involves making some difficult choices which may affect not just you but also your partner, children, business colleagues, even your choice of medical practitioner.

Change also inevitably involves giving something up which, like any bad habit, has become so comfortable you don't immediately recognise how disempowering it is. But, as a Nepalese good luck mantra, advises: 'Judge your success by what you had to give up in order to get it.'

Change, because it involves some kind of loss, incurs a set of typical reactions associated with grieving. First there is *denial* – for example, not accepting that if you want a more secure financial future you will need to sacrifice certain extravagances, at least in the short term. Or that if you are to attract your emotional, intellectual, spiritual and financial equal into your life you need to distance yourself from a partner who locks you into co-dependency.

Look again at your futurelife chart and choose one life area below the central line – an area, in other words, in which you have expressed some current negativity – and ask yourself:

- What choices and decisions did I make in the past, and am I making in the present, that have led me to this situation?

- Why did I make those choices and decisions out of all the ones available to me? Did I really explore all the possibilities or – in retrospect – do I recognise that I made do with the ones that were most immediately apparent?

- What new choices and decisions do I need to make to change my course to the future I want?

- What attitudes/behaviours/beliefs/person/people/ situations do I need to give up in order to change my life for the better?

- How can I make moving towards a fulfilling future in that area more compelling than maintaining the status quo?

- What or who am I afraid of in connection with making these changes?

- How else am I limiting myself?
- What's the worst thing that could happen if I embraced those changes now, and how would I best deal with that scenario if it occurred?
- To what extent do I really believe I can maintain the present as it is and still attract a more spiritually rewarding future?
- What examples have there been in my life so far in which desired change has come about without my doing or thinking differently?

If you really want to expand your life, as well as tuning into your superconscious mind, get into the habit of exercising your brain. There are so many more choices available to you – you just have to think 'out of the box' more. Look for books on enhancing your creativity, which often contain assumption-busting exercises that will also help you expand your life choices.

When you realise that the commitment to change involves making some uncomfortable choices, there is bound to be some sort of accompanying *emotional* response. For example, I was deeply unhappy at the realisation that, in order to have a truly fulfilling relationship with a man, I had to take time out to be by myself, have a relationship with myself and so discover what I really wanted in a partner. When I want something I tend to want it now – not tomorrow or some time in an unspecified future. Therefore I first had to explore why I was so desperate to hang on to the first reasonable relationship that presented itself instead of waiting for a truly meaningful one, and came to the conclusion that I had developed a poverty mentality where men were concerned. I didn't believe there were enough men out there of the calibre I really wanted and felt I deserved. To save myself disappointment and loneliness I had got into the habit of leaping into relationships with men I wouldn't have bothered with had they been women.

Even with this insight I was angry, then sad, then dismayed at the prospect of being by myself for ever. Finally – because any shadowy fear is less terrifying when brought into the light – I understood that the sooner I got to know myself, the sooner I might attract the right man into my life. But at this stage I had only bought into an intellectual understanding. I still had not accepted it.

All of this involved some *resistance* to seeing my situation in a balanced light, which is the next stage of the self-change process. In a moment of despair I decided to opt out of a social life: God was making my life unnecessarily painful, so I was taking my metaphorical ball out of the park and wasn't going to play any more. Luckily my friends wouldn't stand for this self-pitying behaviour and soon got me to snap out of it. But be aware of the self-sabotaging and dysfunctional behaviours and attitudes – particularly centred around blame – that accompany any life-changing process.

Next comes *acceptance*, which is covered in more depth in Chapter 6 where we shall look at the concept of non-attachment. Acceptance comes not just from kicking an idea around for long enough, but from taking actions to prove yourself wrong. Believe me, life isn't designed to keep kicking you in the teeth, and the new opportunities that will start presenting themselves to you will turn out to be much more desirable than what you had become rooted into.

The final part of this process occurs when you demonstrate a *commitment* to doing everything you can to make the changes in your life as wonderful as possible for all concerned. Having had this communication with your Higher Self you develop the ability to communicate more effectively with others, being honest about the changes you intend to bring about, when they are likely to happen and how this might affect everyone else. Then you begin to see, magically, that those other people who are affected by your new choices recognise the value – the wisdom – of that change too.

Dream Exercise 2: Push–Pull Balancing

This exercise has been developed from a concept known as force-field analysis, in which researchers analyse the stresses in any given material and discover what they have to do to counterbalance them. In human situations, too, there are positive and negative forces at work – those that drive us forward and towards our goals, and those that try to restrain us.

Looking again at your futurelife chart, take one of the negative area statements that you have entered below the central line. Then identify a current situation from that area that you wish to change positively and write that down in the middle of the sheet. For example, from the personal finances sector Sandy, a newly divorced woman with a reasonably paid but insecure portfolio career, had written: 'I am using my credit cards beyond my ability to clear the balance every month.'

Underneath that sentence, examine six to eight beneficial forces that will move that negative situation towards an ideal outcome. Similarly, above your sentence highlight six to eight restraining forces that are maintaining the undesired status quo. From the above example, Sandy identified the following:

Restraining Forces

1. I'm a shopaholic. When I see something I want I buy it on credit, with no regard to how I'm going to pay for it in the end.
2. My income doesn't match the lifestyle I'd been used to when I lived with my husband, and I resent that.
3. I'm still angry at Peter for leaving me so financially insecure and I think I'm trying to make him suffer by near-bankrupting myself – when in fact I'm the one who is paying financially and psychologically for these actions.
4. I believe I'm incapable of handling money responsibly.
5. I don't want to handle everything by myself (that's why

I got married to Peter), so spending money is my escape.
6. My income isn't regular enough for me to be able to organise my finances properly.
7. I don't have the motivation to check my income and outgoings regularly.

Driving Forces

1. I love my house and car and don't want to lose them.
2. Having County Court Judgments against me as a bad debtor would detrimentally affect my plans to expand my business.
3. Success is a far more satisfying way of getting my revenge on Peter than financial failure.
4. I need to boost my income, and in particular to find several more sources of good, regular money.
5. My best friend has gone from success to success since her divorce. I want to be like Mary, and she's willing to offer advice on how to manage my finances better.
6. I handled money well when I was a teenager, saving enough to buy my own car at eighteen. If I could do it then, I can do it now – I've just got out of the habit.
7. I don't get any real enjoyment from the things I buy under the current circumstances. I'd rather wait, save up and occasionally splash out on something really special – that would be more of a treat.
8. Handling my personal finances more effectively will give me the skills and confidence I need to expand my business.

In the same way that Shadows present golden opportunities to learn more fulfilling ways of living our lives (see p. 32), this exercise provided Sandy with fifteen opportunities to recognise and overcome dysfunctional attitudes and behaviours. This enabled her to identify the positive actions she needed to take in order to bring closer every day the glorious future she had visualised for herself.

Now use this force-field analysis exercise in each of the specific areas that you wish to change, and discover for yourself just how many options you have when you highlight both the driving and restraining forces at play.

Change and Continuity

Every day our bodies change, yet stay the same. We maintain a cohesive framework despite the fact that we get a new stomach lining every five days, a new skin once a month, a new liver every six weeks and four new skeletons a year. This is consistent with the Yin–Yang concept explored in Chapter 1 (see p. 29). The body makes these changes effortlessly, while supporting the principle of continuity. Yet when we are faced with making changes they can seem insurmountable. This is another situation where tension creeps in, leading us to feel so overwhelmed that it seems better to do nothing at all. Here's a technique to help you appreciate that quite fundamental changes can be made simply by breaking them down into small, incremental stages. It is based on a puzzle you probably played as a child, in which you change one word into another by altering one letter each time. For example, you can change 'cat' into 'dog' in the following stages: cat, cot, cog, dog.

Dream Exercise 3: Creative Changes

Draw two oval shapes, one at the bottom and one at the top of a blank sheet of paper. Between them draw a number of large, square boxes. In the top oval write a new attitude, behaviour or situation that you want to achieve. In the bottom oval write one thing that you feel is disempowering you right now. Starting from the bottom of the paper, identify one small change that you can make today that will move you towards your desired outcome. As with the word example above, make sure each new change leads on from the last one. For instance:

Old Situation

I'm in a dead-end job I hate.

New Situation

I have a job I feel passionate about.

Stages

- I'm in a dead-end job I hate. . . .
- I'll buy a book/go on a course on finding work I love . . .
- and do the exercises on a regular basis . . .
- to rediscover all the things I'm passionate about and find a pattern . . .
- then link that pattern to work and identify what really motivates me . . .
- which will help me identify the kinds of jobs that would allow me to express myself fully . . .
- and identify what new skills or qualifications, if any, I need . . .
- so I can take steps to acquire those skills or qualifications . . .
- then identify which organisations are offering the kind of work I want . . .
- and let them know about me (i.e. send out my CV) . . .
- so I can arrange interviews and use all the feedback to improve my chances to be offered my ideal work . . .
- but I will only make my final choice based on what I have learned about myself . . .
- so that: I have a job I feel passionate about.

Depending on whatever it is you want to change, this exercise may involve a few steps or many. Nevertheless, if you are committed to making lasting, fulfilling changes to your life this is an ideal way of becoming less overwhelmed by what lies ahead. Chapter 5 explains how to set realistic time-frames in which to achieve each of the incremental steps you've highlighted.

Flesh on the Bones

Shortly you will be composing a vision statement that will move you even more quickly from where you are to where you want to be. That's because, while thoughts are power-ful energetic forces, the very act of writing them down gives them a measure of reality in the here and now.

You need to avoid the tired clichés of businesses which get management consultants to write 'mission statements' for them that sound impressive but have no basis in day-to-day reality. That's why I ask you to take time out now to redo the 'baggage' visualisation (see p. 74) and then revisit your personal labyrinth in your mind's eye. Doodling labyrinths and tracing your finger along the pathways will also help clear your mind of extraneous and limiting thoughts.

Dream Pathway 3 is taking us closer to the action part of the process and is therefore concerned with embracing new attitudes, beliefs and behaviours. What underpins all these things are your values. Until you know what these core motivations or guiding principles are, you will continue to make decisions or take actions that cause you inner conflict rather than completion and wholeness.

Dream Exercise 4: the Five Whys

Sometimes it is difficult to know exactly what your values are, which is why this exercise is so useful. Select one posi-tive aspect of your current life from the futurelife chart – one of the things that you did not visualise changing in the future – and frame it like an affirmation (a powerful short sentence that will help positively reframe your mental messages). This example can come from any of the sections, and you can use this process with other life areas to expand or affirm your list of core values.

When you have written this living affirmation on a blank sheet of paper, start to ask yourself why you do what you do and go on until you begin to get to the core of who you are. For example, you may have written 'I am passionate about my work', if this is an area of your life you do not wish to change in any way. One client for whom this was true answered like this:

I am Passionate About my Work

Why? Because I am good and successful at it – I make a lot of money.

Why? It just feels natural and 'right'. My work uses all my skills, traditional and interpersonal.

Why? Because my work reflects who I am as a person, not just what I do.

Why? Because I feel I have a God-given talent that I must express to help others, as well as myself.

Why? I suppose I feel this is about more than work – it's like my life's mission.

On a conscious level, this woman had explained her love of her work materialistically: she was passionate about what she did because of the tangible rewards it brought. But on a much deeper level making money was not a core value at all in her life – having a sense of 'destiny' was. When this knowledge was applied to other areas of her life, she began listening more to her intuition – that inner homing device that (if you're prepared to act on it) will lead you towards greater financial success as well as to emotional and spiritual fulfilment.

Try this exercise for yourself now and see what guiding principles are highlighted for you. Make no judgement, at this stage, about what your core values are. Money and tangible rewards, power and influence, physical comfort, recognition/approbation may be as important to you as altruism, family, sociability or creativity. Get out of the habit of judging the life choices of yourself or others. It is only because of the diversity of life that our experiences have the potential to be so rich.

Dream Exercise 5: the Vision for my Future Life

Now it's time to construct that vision statement I mentioned earlier. This tangible piece of evidence will act as a daily reminder of your destination, and contains everything you need to keep your life on a meaningful, fulfilling course. If it is authentic it will be as relevant in ten years' time as it is today. That is because, while the situations in which you apply them change, your core values – the inner purpose of your life – never do. For this exercise you will need:

- Your completed futurelife chart
- A list of at least ten core values that are relevant to some or all of the nine life sectors listed on your futurelife chart
- A book of speeches by leading historical figures (such as *The Penguin Book of Historic Speeches* edited by Brian MacArthur)
- A piece of coloured, lined card that will fit into your suit pocket, handbag or diary so that you have access to it daily

From each of the nine (or more) sectors on your futurelife chart, select one positive affirmation that encapsulates the new course you are committed to travelling. For example: (*health*) 'I have the necessary mental and physical strength to live life to the full'; (*environment*) 'I live in a beautiful, inspiring home in a caring and tolerant society'; (*work*) 'I express myself authentically in work that adds value to other people's lives as well as mine and my family's.'

Once you have your nine statements, look at how you can change some of the phrasing to include mention of your core values, in terms of either actual words or the spirit of their meaning. Here are some snippets from a number of enlightened corporate vision statements that combine vision and values:

- Nickelodeon (US children's cable channel): To make kids feel good about themselves.

- Marriott Hotels: To make guests feel special.

- Sony: To experience the joy of producing technologies that benefit the general public.

- Wal-Mart: To make shoppers' lives better via lower prices and greater selectivity.

- Disney: To bring happiness to millions.

- Philip Morris: To defend the right to personal freedom of choice.

Finally, consider how you can combine these nine mini-statements to make a cohesive, inspiring vision statement for your life. Look at the way great orators such as Martin Luther King, Winston Churchill and John F. Kennedy articulated words that captured people's hearts, not just their minds. Consider the passion, symbolism, use of metaphor and visual imagery of lines like these:

> *I know I have the body of a weak and feeble woman, but I have the heart and stomach of a king, and a King of England too.*
>
> Queen Elizabeth I of England, 1588

> *Your country therefore calls upon me to cleanse this Augean stables. . . .*
>
> Oliver Cromwell, 1653

> *The mystic chords of memory, stretching from every battlefield and patriot grave to every living heart and hearthstone all over this broad land, will yet swell the chorus of the Union, when again touched as surely they will be, by the better angels of our nature.*
>
> Abraham Lincoln, 1861

Let us therefore brace ourselves to our duties and so bear ourselves that, if the British Empire and its Commonwealth last for a thousand years, men will still say: 'This was their finest hour.'

Winston Churchill, 1940

My fellow citizens of the world: ask not what America will do for you, but what together we can do for the freedom of man.

John F. Kennedy, 1961

When we let freedom ring, when we let it ring from every village and every hamlet, from every state and every city, we will be able to speed up that day when all of God's children, black men and white men, Jews and Gentiles, Protestants and Catholics, will be able to join hands and sing in the words of the old Negro spiritual, 'Free at last! free at last! thank God Almighty, we are free at last!'

Martin Luther King, 1963

If you are really committed to a glorious future for yourself, use appropriately inspiring, emotion-filled words to describe it. Let your creative juices flow – this vision statement is for your eyes only, so there is no need to be shy about it. Even if you are more used to writing shopping lists, explore how inspired and imaginative you can be with words when you are operating from your Higher Self.

When you have composed a vision statement that fills you with excitement and pride, write it down on the card and keep it with you at all times. Look at the card every day – when you get up in the morning and just before you settle down for the night. As you journey towards a life of inner fulfilment and joy, these words will powerfully keep your bearings true.

And now, the call to action. . . .

5

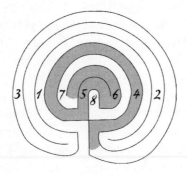

THE DO OR ACTION
PATHWAYS

*Inspiration may be a form of superconsciousness or
perhaps subconsciousness – I wouldn't know. But I
am sure it is the antithesis of self-consciousness.*

Aaron Copland, twentieth-century American composer

*We don't see things as they are, we see things as we
are.*

Anaïs Nin, twentieth-century French writer

The Labyrinth Visualisation *Part 2*

*Now it's time to enter the first of the Do pathways . . .
Pathway 4. . . the pathway of change. . . . Because the
purpose of this pathway is concerned with changing behaviour,
think about one thing you will commit to doing differently
today . . . right now . . . that will begin to make your
most fulfilled future a reality. . . . There is no need to wait
until you have effectively changed your thoughts before
you take this action. . . . Ask your Higher Self what it is you
need to do to make that change a reality . . . now. . . .*

(Pause for ten seconds.)

You will shortly be coming to the entrance to Pathway

5. . . . This is the shortest pathway. . . . Slow yourself down as you come to it. . . . Be aware of your breathing. . . . Relax your body and mind even more deeply as you move further into the labyrinth. . . . Imagine that in the middle of this short pathway is a puddle of water. . . . What does it feel like to run your finger through this tiny pool? . . . Imagine you are looking into the dark water. . . . Your reflection is looking back at you as you ask: 'What do I need to know to overcome the challenges between where I am and where I am meant to be? . . . What do I know about my mission in life that I thought I didn't know?' . . . The fluidity of this puddle of water offers a flash of inspiration, a gut feeling, a creative hunch that is relevant to your journey. . . . You are aware of it now. . . .

(Pause for ten seconds.)

Be clear about what intuition you have been offered before you move on . . . slipping into Pathway 6 – the pathway of diversity. . . .

In this sixth pathway, which is slightly longer but slopes even more deeply downwards than the last, you become aware of a shrouded figure. . . . This is your mystery mentor . . . someone whose attitude, behaviour, gifts, life history . . . are a source of inspiration to you. . . . Who is this person? . . . Male or female . . . it could be someone you know or do not know . . . someone living or not living. . . . Be aware of them . . . now. . . .

Action-packed

When you are wholeheartedly focused on excavating your divine purpose in order to find lasting fulfilment in your life, you will be prepared to take appropriate action. Indeed, one of the key pieces of advice I give my coaching clients is to stop thinking so much about what they are going to do and just do it. This has been called 'acting one's way into a new way of thinking', and can produce quicker results than spending hours intellectualising and theorising. Having travelled the dream pathways, you should have a golden vision to aim for. Now it's time to put your plan into action.

The benefit of 'acting one's way into thinking' is illustrated in an anecdote told by the theatre director Richard Olivier, son of the famous actor Lord Olivier. While studying in America, Richard was in an acting class in which the teacher asked one of the students to come through a door and slam it to indicate that he was angry. The young actor tried several times, without success, finally complaining to the director that he couldn't do so because he didn't *feel* angry. 'Slam the door, and then you will!' came the reply.

What this story highlights is that to be successful in your endeavours – indeed, to produce quicker results than trying to get your head around a particular challenge – appropriate action has to come before thought. You will notice that I use the words 'appropriate action'. Ancient wisdom teaches that inside each one of us is the key to understanding everything that has ever happened, is happening or will happen in the future. Another advantage of tweaking our innate radio dials so that we are properly tuned into messages from the universe or Divine Guidance is that we enhance our intuition, the 'gut instincts' or internal antennae that guide us to take the right action at the right time. The exercise on p. 102 will give you a flavour of just how acute your intuition is.

One of the greatest inhibitors of right action is the fear of making mistakes, of 'failing' and of appearing foolish to others as a result. If this fear has debilitated you in the past, you might like to reflect upon the words of the nineteenth-century author of *Self-Help*, Samuel Smiles, who wrote: 'We learn wisdom from failure much more than from success. We often discover what will do by finding out what will not do; and probably he who never made a mistake never made a discovery.'

You might also like to reflect on how hard we adults are on ourselves. As small children, over a relatively short period of time, we had to learn how to walk, talk, stay safe, make friends and please our parents. Not one of us managed to pick ourselves up from the floor one day and walk across a room without stumbling and falling. That's because walking was a new skill and we had to make a lot of slips and miscalculations before we mastered it. Frankly, life is no different for adults – except that the skills we are embracing are of a more self-revelatory and interpersonal nature. Stop thinking you have to get everything perfect all the time. When faced with a new situation, there is more chance of your getting things wrong than of getting them right. The beauty of the situation is that you will learn fast how to do it differently next time.

CASE HISTORY: Stephen's Story

It is a good idea to get into the habit of framing whatever situation you find yourself in as a positive, not as a negative. The advantage of this was highlighted to a client of mine who, during an early coaching session, had produced a long list of disadvantages. One of these was 'limited reputation'. Stephen felt that if more people knew about him, and if his status within his profession was perceived by others as being higher, he wouldn't be facing so many problems with his business. The fact was that Stephen didn't want to be shackled to his current business any more and was looking to diversify. Therefore his 'limited reputation' was a benefit, since he hadn't been pigeonholed or typecast into one particular role. Also, having realised that he hadn't exploited his skills and promoted his business as effectively as he could have in the past, Stephen recognised that marketing was something he needed to focus on more in the future.

The first of the action pathways involves you highlighting one behaviour that you are committed to changing right now. Hence the first exercise of this chapter is a straightforward one.

Do/Action Exercise 1: Do It Now

Whether it's signing up for that exercise class to improve your fitness, volunteering for community work, clearing the clutter from your home or office, or building bridges with estranged members of your family – do it now.

Then, when you have taken that first step, consider all the other changes you need to make to become the balanced, fulfilled, successful individual you viewed on your futurelife screen. For each required life change complete Dream Exercise 3 (p. 92), which sets out the incremental steps you must take in order to move from where you are to where you want to be. Then set a realistic time-frame for each of those steps. Don't make these so short that you are constantly missing deadlines and therefore become dispirited. Nor, on the other hand, should they be too long, which would indicate that each small change is low on your list of priorities. A useful technique is to set a date by which you intend to have made the highlighted change, and then work backwards.

Passion, Pondering or Procrastination?

There are plenty of books that will help you manage your time more effectively and schedule new tasks into your daily timetable. Even so, while the common advice of time management experts is the 3 Ds (Do, Defer or Delegate), in my experience most people who are faced with the daunting prospect of making major changes to their lives end up displaying the 3 Ps: Passion, Pondering or Procrastination. I define these as:

Passion

Knowing what you want at the deepest level of your being, and therefore having the motivation to achieve them.

Pondering

Not knowing exactly how you want your life to be yet, but committing the time and energy to exploring all the possibilities.

Procrastination

Thinking you know what you want, but finding that you constantly put off taking any sort of action to bring about change.

Venturing into the labyrinth and completing the exercises in Chapter 4 are designed to help you with the first two Ps: finding your passion and unpacking what it is you really want your life to be like. However, if, after highlighting those things on which you need to take action you find that you are not motivated enough to move yourself forward, this may be for two reasons.

Firstly, you may not have journeyed into the labyrinth in an altered state of consciousness, which is the only state in which you can begin to access the heartfelt desires of your Higher Self. Changes that are invested with a deeper meaning and purpose are so compelling that it is virtually impossible not to carry them out. Secondly, any form of inaction or resistance to change suggests a fear attached to it that has not been addressed. And whatever fear you uncover highlights a key action that you need to take before trying to make other changes. Here is an exercise to help you identify what is blocking you from taking appropriate action.

Do/Action Exercise 2: Procrastination Patterns

List ten things that you habitually put off doing. If you know you are a regular procrastinator, or if other people have accused you of being one, you may not need to go back more than a few weeks or months to find your examples. If you only occasionally put off taking action in certain areas of your life, you may need to go back further in your memory.

When you have your ten examples, look for a pattern. Perhaps they all belong in a specific area of your life. Many people procrastinate when it comes to personal finances, for instance not regularly balancing their cheque books against their bank statements, never getting around to sorting out a personal pension or life assurance, or having no idea of their monthly outgoings and therefore always finding themselves in debt.

Others find that their list is concerned with a particular type of inaction, such as phone fear. This is a common self-sabotage mechanism for many of my self-employed coaching clients, who find themselves intimidated by the thought of pitching new ideas to decision-makers or even following up introductory letters with a telephone call. Actions that you don't want to take, but have to, represent the worst case scenario of time management. These are the things that remain on your To Do list for months on end, nagging at you like a toothache and constantly reminding you that you are not as effective as you could be.

So, what action can you take? For a start you could try the five whys exercise (Dream Exercise 4 on p. 97) to help you identify the nature of this mental blockage. Here's an example of how this works (and, as you can see, you often don't even need to get to the fifth 'Why?' before the solution becomes apparent):

Self-Sabotaging Fear

I'm intimidated by 'cold calling' on the telephone.

Why? Because I always make such a mess of it – stumbling over words and being gripped by fear.

Why? Because I don't know how to articulate myself quickly and effectively over the telephone.

Why? Because I've never had any training in this area.

If you want to establish and sustain a new belief, you need to furnish yourself with the skills that make it possible. In the above example, my client Joe recognised that he needed to find out how successful salespeople made sales calls over the telephone. So he booked a course and armed himself with techniques that boosted his confidence as well as his skills, and as a result he has never since had any problem picking up the telephone to prospective clients. It wasn't that Joe didn't have the capability – he had simply never learned how.

When you are gripped by a fear that stops you taking action, you have absorbed a false belief about yourself. That false belief is usually based on a lack of skill. If you want to become skilful in something, you need advice or training. Then, and only then, can you script a new, empowering belief – and no longer be a slave to procrastination.

Nine times out of ten I find that the inaction of my clients is underpinned by some kind of fear. However, if you are unable to identify a phobia connected with your procrastination about something you believe you are committed to changing, I suggest you undertake the preparatory and labyrinth visualisations again. This time make sure to relax your body and mind even more deeply, as the insights you gleaned first time may have come more from your conscious mind or ego rather than from your Higher Self.

Exploring With Others

Doing need not be a lonely process. We have access not only to Divine Guidance but to the perspectives and experience of others, from which we can learn to expand and enrich our lives. The rest of this chapter highlights ways in which you can learn to benefit from the wisdom and experience of others – known as well as unknown to you, dead or alive.

Do/Action Exercise 3: New Dimensions

There is a Buddhist saying, 'A man cannot see his own eyebrows.' Similarly, we have a natural tendency to undervalue our skills and talents because we have taken them for granted. There are four actual or potential areas of self-knowledge:

1. What you and other people know about you.
2. What other people know about you that you don't know.

3. What you know about yourself that others don't know.
4. What is hidden from everyone (untapped potential).

The Dream pathways and exercises in Chapter 4 have been designed to help you expand the self-knowledge of areas 1 and 3. Area 4 will be looked at in a later exercise, but for now let's examine area 2.

This exercise is based on one that my own life coach required me to do in order to expand my awareness of myself and the gifts that I was perhaps not fully understanding or appreciating. It proved incredibly illuminating and helpful to me, as I'm sure it will be for you.

Write or type the following questions on to a sheet of paper, leaving enough space between each for a short answer:

- What are my strengths?

- What are my understrengths (a more empowering word than 'weaknesses')?

- What aspect of our friendship do you appreciate most?

- What talents/skills do I have that you most admire, yet I seem to undervalue?

- What talents do you recognise in me that I don't appear to realise I have?

- What do you think I need most that I'm not currently getting?

- What one thing would you change about me?

- In what area(s) do you think I would benefit from more training and development?

- What would you be willing to give me that I have never asked you for?

- What untapped potential do you believe I have which you haven't even thought about until now?

The questions are deliberately general so that they don't immediately suggest a particular answer. Make copies and give them to five close, supportive friends, asking them to answer the questions in an open and honest way. Tell them that this self-knowledge exercise is for your use only, and there will be no comeback on anything that they write. Unless there is a point that needs clarification, it is best not to engage in any further discussion of this questionnaire. Bear in mind that whatever people write is how they view you. If you read something you are uncomfortable with, this does not mean that your friends are criticising you but that you have been presented with the perfect opportunity to address an issue that hitherto you weren't aware of and may be detrimentally affecting your relationship with others.

CASE HISTORY: Beverley's Story

Beverley found that, despite giving this questionnaire to five very different people, she received similar answers. Apart from getting a boost from reading all the positive things her friends had to say about her, some of the insights proved to be very powerful in helping her see that she was 'repeat offending' with inappropriate attitudes and behaviours. This was particularly true in one area that had caused Beverley a lot of pain and distress – her tendency to choose weak, unsuitable partners. Although her original focus for this exercise had been her work, the answers emphasised how capable and strong her friends perceived her to be, and how distressed they were when they saw Beverley wasting her time on dysfunctional child-men.

When we discussed her friends' very different perception of Beverley's abilities to her own, it became apparent that this bright, bubbly, compelling woman was replaying an old life script based on how she had been as a child and not on how she was today. Over time she mentally mixed up the naturally protective way she dealt with her six younger brothers with they way she felt she needed to be with her lovers. Beverley subconsciously chose men who needed 'fixing' in a big-sisterly way and then wondered why – after she had poured a lot of time, money and effort into their lives and careers – they left her for partners whom they could relate to as desirable, sexy women and not as a sibling.

Once Beverley acknowledged this habit she became more adept at spotting men with more emotional baggage than she was prepared to take on board. She also began to focus more on her own career, and redirected the effort she normally channeled towards the men in her life towards her own fulfilment.

When you have studied the answers you get from this questionnaire, look at the contrast between how your friends see you and how you perceive yourself. Then try and identify where you may be disempowering yourself with false beliefs about yourself. Once you have done this, it's time to script new, more empowering beliefs as a precursor to formulating new actions and behaviours in the form of affirmations.

Changing Habits

> Habit is either the best of servants or the worst of masters.
>
> Revd Nathaniel Emmons 1745–1840, Honorary Vice President, the American Society for Educating Pious Youth for the Gospel Ministry

It has been estimated that 80 per cent of our behaviour is based on habit, the adaptive knowledge we accrue throughout life in order to prepare ourselves for coping with what life requires us to handle in the future. Instead of reacting authentically, according to how we feel at the time, our habits are like cloaks we wear to protect ourselves from what we perceive as undesirable change. Unfortunately, we may only have had one or two bad experiences before we formed self-protective habits that may no longer be helping us take advantage of new circumstances and a new way of being.

But developing new habits can feel awkward at first. Try these brief exercises:

1. Fold your arms as you would normally. Notice which hand is resting under or on which arm. Then try to refold your arms the reverse way. For example, if your left hand is resting on your right arm with your right hand tucked underneath the left arm, change it so that your right hand is resting on your left arm with the left hand tucked underneath the right arm.
2. Clasp your hands. (Most people will rest their left thumb on the right one.) Now unclasp your fingers and interlace them differently, so that not only is the right thumb resting on the left one but your fingers are interlocking differently from the first time.
3. Pick up a pen. If you are right-handed, try signing your name with your left hand; or with your right hand if you are left-handed.

How comfortable did the 'new' way of folding your arms, clasping your hands or writing your name feel? How often would you need to repeat these exercises before the new habits began to feel like second nature? Certainly not after just a few repetitions, that's for sure. This is why you have to accept the discomfort of change and try to persist with it in the short to medium term.

Now, imagine for a moment you are standing at the edge of a field of grass that reaches up to your knees. The quickest way to get to your destination is through that field and so you decide to cross it. The next day when you retrace your steps the chances are you will not be able to see where you originally crossed because the grass will have sprung up again. But if you were to walk exactly the same route, day in day out, gradually you would wear down the grass until a pathway appeared. Suddenly you wouldn't have to concentrate at all on where you are going because the path would be laid out in front of you.

This is analogous to the way the neural pathways – the biochemical electromagnetic connections between brain cells with each thought or memory – in the brain are strengthened and deepened by habits. If you regularly repeat a positive thought or behaviour you will not only have created a new, more empowering neural connection but you will eventually turn it into a superhighway of changed habits. That's why correctly framed affirmations work so well. Here's how to construct ones that will work for you, based on the template devised by a nineteenth-century French physician, Emil Coué, whose 'cure by auto-suggestion' involved his patients saying repeatedly: 'Every day in every way I am getting better and better.'

Do/Action Exercise 4: Writing Personal Affirmations

1. Identify one or more false beliefs related to those future-life areas that you have written below the line on your chart (see p. 87) and are now committed to changing.
2. Consider what new beliefs you need to embrace in order to support the new reality you are creating for yourself.
3. Beginning each sentence with 'Every day in every way . . .' or simply 'I am . . .', construct a short, positive, action-oriented statement that expresses this new belief. Here are some examples:

- *False belief*: I will never find someone who loves me.
- *New belief*: I am learning to love myself and, in doing so, become more lovable to others.

- *False belief*: I am hopeless with money.
- *New belief*: Every day in every way I am becoming more adept at handling my finances.

- *False belief*: My life is full of disappointments and unhappiness.
- *New belief*: I am gradually recognising the lessons and therefore advantages of everything that happens to me.

- *False belief:* I can't handle change.
- *New belief:* I am increasingly open to recognising and embracing the benefits of the change and ambiguity in my life.

4. Write each of these affirmations on a card as well as in your journal. Create a ritual for yourself which involves reading your affirmations out loud or to yourself first thing in the morning and last thing at night. Wherever possible, carry this card with you and read your affirmations several times during the day. If you think you might forget to do this, get into the habit of pulling out your affirmations card every time you reach for a cup of coffee or a cigarette or eat a meal.

5. Experts estimate that it takes twenty-eight days of daily repetition to develop a new habit. So commit yourself to stating your new beliefs affirmations for a whole month – and just watch how miraculously things begin to change for you.

Handling Your Hunches

The fifth of the labyrinth pathways is concerned with intuition. This innate faculty goes by a number of names such as 'sixth sense', 'gut instinct', 'inner guidance' and 'hunch'. Tony Buzan, one of the world's foremost experts on the brain and creativity, calls it SuperLogic. Whichever term you prefer, the fact is that we all have access to this wellspring of wisdom. Intuition is commonly associated with people who demonstrate enhanced creativity and genius. Why? Such people have not only trained themselves to recognise an intuitive response to life's challenges, but take the action required to reap the benefits. The word intuition comes from the Latin *intueor*, meaning 'to see'; however, this perception does not come from our physical eyes or logical mind. And the reason why many people have trouble accepting and acting on the concept of intuition is precisely that: the insights arrived at in this way aren't

based on anything concrete or logical. Operating principally from the linear, left-brained, masculine part of the
brain, they are distrustful of anything that doesn't bear the
stamp of rationality. I suspect, too, that many men dislike
being associated with some of the feminine traits that
society has combined within the term 'female intuition'.

Ironically, some of the most successful businesspeople
are comfortable using their intuition to make decisions
about a person or situation. When asked, they say they
took action based on nothing more concrete than 'It just
felt right.' Studies conducted at Harvard Business School
have found that senior executives of some of the world's
biggest organisations attribute 80 per cent of their success
to having acted on their intuition or gut feelings. And with
all the recent debate about Emotional Intelligence (EQ),
many business magazines have explored the greater success
in today's marketplace of high-EQ executives as opposed to
those who merely have a high IQ but few, if any, discernible
interpersonal skills.

One of the most common reasons why my clients tell me
they don't act more frequently on their intuition is that they
believe their 'hunches' are more likely to result in failure
and disappointment than choices and actions based on logical evidence. I don't agree and the exercise on p. 120 may
help you dispel that belief for yourself. But first let me offer
a personal example that illustrates how professionally valuable acting on your intuition can be.

CASE HISTORY: Liz's Story

During a particularly worrying career hiatus I was looking to
expand my consultancy services in order to bring in some
much-needed money, and was talking to a number of
organisations about how we might work together. One of
them was a new, exciting, IT-based business and, having
met a couple of their executives in a separate capacity, I
arranged a meeting with their CEO. This man was perfectly
pleasant and very keen on getting me to work with them in

a freelance capacity. Indeed, he pushed me to draw up a contract before I left for my Christmas holiday. But there was something about him that made me feel uneasy. I couldn't put my finger on it – after all, the deal was likely to be a good one (as I was largely penning it) and here was the answer to my prayers as far as interesting, value-creating, well-paid work was concerned.

Having ignored my intuition on several occasions and lived to regret it, I did something totally illogical – and not entirely truthful. I told the CEO that my focus had changed, that an unexpected two-book deal had been presented to me and that I wouldn't be able to give his business the time and attention it deserved if I attempted both kinds of work. So I was bowing out gracefully. He wrote me a very courteous e-mail reply wishing me luck – and within a month I had received the two-book deal which, when I had mentioned it to him, was still wishful thinking.

Not long afterwards I was contacted by another executive who had left the company; he told me that a large number of senior staff had decided to resign. Although on the face of it the company appeared successful, there was never enough money to pay the salaries that had been agreed at their interviews. Had I ignored my intuition, and been recruited by this inefficient and dishonest CEO, I too would have found myself spending valuable time on projects for which I never got paid.

Cosmic Web – or Internal Storage?

Considering that over 50 per cent of people questioned in the UK and US claim to have psychic or otherwise inexplicable experiences, including success from 'hunches', this phenomenon is not something that can be ignored – particularly when your goal is a life of total fulfilment. Joanna Kozubska states in *The 7 Keys of Charisma* that charismatic people – those remarkable inspirational individuals whose lives often seem 'charmed' – are those who operate largely on instinct and intuition.

In his book *The Luck Factor*, Max Gunther points out

that 'lucky' people are a breed who trust and act on their intuitions. Gunther relates the story of hotelier Conrad Hilton, who was one of a number of individuals aiming to buy a hotel for sale in Chicago. The property would be sold to whoever offered the highest sealed bid. Hilton had entered a bid of $165,000 but, a few nights before the deadline, woke with a strong hunch that this was not enough and as a result upped his bid to $180,000. Hilton was successful – and discovered that the next bid down was for $179,800. Had he not acted on that gut instinct, he would have lost his prize.

Another story involves Jesse Livermore, a famous US speculator at the turn of the twentieth century who, against all logical explanation, acted on a hunch. He took the risky action of short selling thousands of shares in Union Pacific, one of the hottest stocks on the market at the time. Short selling meant that if the stock price fell he would make money, but if it rose he would likely bankrupt himself. The day after he did so, San Francisco was ravaged by an earthquake which buried Union Pacific's offices and with it the earnings potential of that stock. Jesse Livermore became richer by some $300,000.

There are two basic explanations for how or why intuition works. The first is metaphysical, the second more scientific. I invite you to select whichever resonates with you most. We have already explored the quantum notion of a universe in which everything is irrevocably interconnected and thus we all have access to knowledge about everything that has ever been, is, or will be. Hence an intuition is simply a connection with cosmic consciousness via the conduit of the Higher Self. It is only when the chattering 'monkey mind' of the ego is quieted that we can hear the whispers of our innate wisdom, which is why silent meditation and visualisations are so powerful.

Facts Experienced As Feelings

There is a second, more scientific explanation for intuition. Look back at the visualisation instructions relating to

Pathway 5. The key phrase is: 'What do you know about your mission in life that you thought you didn't know?' Tony Buzan suggests that, since the brain is able to make the most amazing mathematical calculations, what we call 'gut feel' is simply a biological reaction based on the vast database of information which has been processed by the brain since the moment you were born, and of which you are not consciously aware.

Intuitions present themselves in many forms – as images or symbols, through dreams, as words, or more commonly as physical sensations and feelings. Our minds analyse the trillions of items of data which are made available to us over a lifetime (or, to someone who believes in past lives, over many lifetimes), not just on the basis of 'facts' but also from our responses to interactions with our external environment. According to US psychologist Dr Eugene Gendlin, those people who live 'lucky' or fulfilled and joyous lives are those who regularly excavate this stratum of subsurface knowledge. The process may bypass your reasoning mind, but that doesn't make it any less valuable.

With regard to the visualisation you experienced on Pathway 5, by asking your subconscious or Higher Self 'What do you know about your mission in life that you thought you didn't know?' while in a state of quiet contemplation you are simply taking advantage of the immense internal cornucopia of emotional knowledge. Through your sixth sense you find out you know something that you didn't know you knew. All that remains for you to do now is to act on that intuitive information.

To rediscover your intuitive self is to excavate a childlike state. Children, not shackled by society's expectations, habitual responses or analytical reasoning, make hunch-based assessments of other people and situations. In their innocence they are much more in tune with the vibrations coming off other people and what adults call 'atmospheres'. If only we adults would listen to them and stop asking for facts to back up their assertions, we would find that children perceive more than they see. As we grow older this innate talent becomes buried under years of socialisation, embarrassment and distrust. The following exercises are designed to help you clear some of that debris and get access to the untapped potential currently hidden from your conscious self and others.

Do/Action Exercise 5: Flexing Your Intuitive Muscle

> *By keeping the feminine way you . . . go back to become as a child.*

Lao Tsu, 6th c. BC Chinese philosopher, one of the founders of Taoism and author of the Tao Te Ching 'The Way'

Start by reviewing the intuition you gained from the Pathway 5 visualisation. Try not to intellectualise it or to find some rational explanation for why it should or should not 'work' for you. Simply ask yourself how you feel about whatever came up for you. Engage in a dialogue with yourself in which you constantly ask questions such as:

- What do I feel about this person/situation?
- Why do these feelings disturb me?
- What might I know about this that I didn't realise I knew?
- Who might I speak to for greater clarification on this?

Always keep your mind on your feelings – first in a big-picture, general sense, and then turn your focus to more specific emotions. Once you have unpacked your intuition in this way as far as you can, determine to act on it if it feels right to do so. If not, go back to Exercise 2 (p. 107) and examine what fears are being highlighted that need to be explored and dealt with first. Either way you win, because you are discovering more and more about the lifelong habits that are sabotaging your chance of finding fulfilment.

Do/Action Exercise 6: Symbolic Synchronicity

The eight-step labyrinth process that I use with my coaching clients is slightly different from the version presented in this book. One of the things I do is encourage clients to visualise a symbol in each of the pathways; we then discuss its meaning in relation to their current situation or challenge. But a symbol-oriented approach presents problems in a book because each symbol has a unique meaning based on the specific life of the individual. However, this exercise will help you explore the value of symbolic guidance from the Higher Self and to become more familiar with the wisdom of symbols. Unlike tarot cards or rune stones which tend to offer meanings according to someone else's insights, this exercise uses everyday items to help you shift your perspective on your problem and enhance your ability to come up with intuitive solutions. It will train you to become more creative in your approach to problems, and present you with far more options than might normally be the case.

Opportunity Clock

This exercise is based on a creativity method called Circle of Opportunity.

1. Decide on an issue from the lower section of your futurelife chart (see p. 87) which you wish to challenge and change. Formulate a general, open-ended question to ask your Higher Self, such as: 'What do I need to know to take the right action?' or 'What do I need to do differently to find the solution to my problem?'
2. Take a moment to calm yourself physically and mentally. Then determine to pick up intuitively an everyday object, something close to you at this moment, which will offer clarification.
3. Trust that whatever you choose will be the right symbol at this time. In line with the infinite connections of the

universe, you *will* find what you are looking for. Go with your first, instinctive response. The only occasions on which this exercise does not work are when clients *think* too hard about it. Leave your logical mind behind and go with your gut feeling.

4. Draw a circle on a page in your journal or on a sheet of paper and divide it into twelve segments, like the five-minute sections of a clock.

5. Place your object in front of you and examine it closely. In each of the twelve segments of your circle, write down one characteristic of that object. For example, if your object is a knife your list might include sharpness, metallic, cold, shiny, reflection, texture, shape, weight.

6. Thinking about the issue on which you want clarification, work your way from the number one position (NNE) through to number twelve and, working with whatever comes into your mind, make connections and relationships between each attribute and your problem.

CASE HISTORY: Howard's Story

Howard had visualised his dream partner, but seemed to do everything in his power not to realise his goal by rarely socialising and failing to ask suitable women out when he did meet them. The object he had intuitively chosen was a cup he had bought in Italy which was suggestive of the Holy Grail, according to legend the cup from which Jesus Christ drank at the Last Supper. It was a jewel-encrusted, weighty article which, although obviously tangible, had a fantasy quality about it. Bought on a whim, it had never really fitted in with the minimalistic décor of Howard's home and he had often thought of giving it to a charity shop except for the fact that it had cost him so much.

We discussed what the characteristics of this cup told Howard about his attitude towards his dream relationship. Was it really so compelling? Howard realised he had a basic fear of his dream becoming reality because he associated it with being weighed down with the responsibility of marriage and parenthood. The Holy Grail connection highlighted his inner belief that such a partnership was a fantasy, out of keeping with the bachelor lifestyle he enjoyed so much. Howard recognised that his dream had more to do with his mother's aspirations for him than with his own. Having realised this, he courageously asked his mother to stop putting pressure on him to find a partner and to get used to the fact that he would probably never present her with grandchildren.

CASE HISTORY: Jane's Story

Throughout her marriage and particularly since her divorce, Jane had suffered from a lack of confidence that was affecting her career prospects as well as her social life and, through stress, her long-term health. Her article was a small shield with crossed swords on a backing of tartan, signifying the Scottish clan to which her family belonged. The attributes which Jane earmarked on her clock included protection, family, history and strength.

While musing about the connections between these concepts and her problem, Jane was inspired to see the most obvious link. She had enjoyed fencing at school and had competed at junior championship level. Acting on this intuition, Jane found a local fencing school and began to go to classes. She rediscovered her fascination with the grace and discipline of this sport, and was delighted to find that she had not lost her natural ability. This not only immediately boosted her confidence but improved her health, as she now had an outlet for her pent-up anger and frustration. It also had an unexpected knock-on benefit for her love life. Jane began to socialise with other members of the fencing club and, through one of them, met her future husband. She says this relationship has been the most fulfilling and equal partnership she has ever had.

Do/Action Exercise 7: The $64,000 Question

This is one of the shortest, simplest but most invaluable exercises for developing your intuition. Whenever you are presented with a problem or situation about which you are confused, ask yourself: 'What do I know about this that I didn't realise I knew?' Then wait for the insights to present themselves to you. Remember, intuitive flashes come in many forms – as words, images, symbols, dreams or feelings. Even if you are not compelled to act on these insights, which have been described as 'the place where artists work', at least make a note of them in your journal. Doing so will enable you to look for patterns and, when reviewing your life in the future, you will be able prove to yourself how valuable intuitions can be in directing you towards the fulfilling life you desire for yourself. The more open you are to taking advantage of this wellspring of knowledge, the easier you will find it to trust in the wisdom of your Higher Self and then take the action necessary to capitalise on those insights.

How Do You Do That?

On the last of the Do or Action pathways you conjured up a shrouded figure, your mystery mentor. The concept of modelling yourself on the attitudes and behaviours of others is used in Neuro Linguistic Programming (NLP), which was developed in the early 1970s as the study of excellence in all its forms. In a research project aimed at discovering why some people were consistently successful, Californians John Grinder and Richard Bandler studied the language and actions of a number of highly admired therapists including Fritz Perls, father of Gestalt therapy, and Virginia Satir.

NLP practitioners uncover all they can about how someone else produces successful results by asking, 'How do you do that?' The rationale is that by eliciting both the conscious and unconscious processes of these mentors, others can adopt them and enjoy the same level of success. I have always had certain objections to NLP, not least that modelling is not authentic. While it may be advantageous to discover how and why someone does what they do so well, I question the validity of taking on another person's thoughts and actions when they might not be consistent with your own core values. However, in line with our appreciation of the interconnectedness of all things, past, present and future, there is no harm in asking the question, 'What would you do?' or 'How would you tackle this problem?' and then making a decision about whether to act on that advice. It is on that basis that this next exercise has been designed.

Do/Action Exercise 8: Mystery Mentor

Begin by finding out everything you can about your mystery mentor. This person may be dead or alive, known or unknown to you. In some ways it is probably easier to research a long-deceased historical figure from books. Wherever possible look for autobiographical works that go beyond the personal proclivities of a journalist or biographer. If your mystery mentor is alive and known to you, I suggest you ask permission to discuss how they do what they do, admitting that you admire them enough to want to embrace some of those processes yourself.

When you really feel you have got under the skin of this person, use that knowledge whenever you are presented with a challenge for which no immediate answer is apparent to you. Go into a deeply relaxed state using any of the visualisations in this book or a meditative technique with which you are comfortable or familiar, and imagine your mentor is sitting in front of you. Conduct a conversation with them about your problem. Ask their advice. Discover what they would do in your situation. Then, using your intuition – that is, being sensitive to your feelings about this advice – assess what action you will take, if any, based on that advice.

Remember, questions hold the key to your future fulfilment. You probably already know the value of discussing problems with friends and family – the old adage of 'a problem shared is a problem halved'. Your mystery mentor – or mentors (you can imagine a whole committee of them, if you like) – are simply another resource to tap into when you are unsure what action to take to turn your dreams into reality. Whether you believe you are really tapping into this person's consciousness, are getting guidance from God or a Higher Power through your imagination, or are 'dreaming up' your own solutions doesn't matter. This technique is simply a way of asking questions in order to expand your choices so that your life is as creatively abundant and fulfilling as possible.

Take advantage of the diversity in your life by asking for a gift from everyone with whom you come into contact. Imagine that life is a universal classroom where each person has something to teach you as well as something to learn from you. When you come across a trait, attitude, characteristic or behaviour that you admire in someone, ask them how they manage to do it – for example, 'How do you manage to stay so cheerful when customers are rude to you?', 'How do you find the courage to chat up someone you've never met before, but would like to know better?' or 'How do you get your doctor to treat you like a human being and not as a symptom?'

And Now. . . .

As we've been focusing in Chapters 4 and 5 on conjuring up our innermost dreams and taking the actions that will make them reality, it might seem paradoxical to detach ourselves from having anything we've done so far come true. But that's exactly what we're going to explore in the next chapter.

6

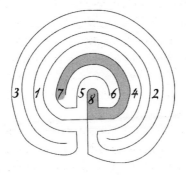

THE DETACH PATHWAYS

All paths lead to and from the centre. Following them is a quest, but at a certain point realising them is an act of surrender.

Danah Zohar, *Spiritual Intelligence*

Ultimately you must forget about techniques. The further you progress the fewer techniques there are. The Great Path is really No Path.

Morihei Ueshiba, *The Art of Peace*

The Labyrinth Visualisation *Part 3*

As you begin to enter the seventh pathway . . . you become aware of the need to be open to new, as yet unknown possibilities. . . . This is the first of the Detach pathways, representing the ability to let go, to detach from specific outcomes and allow the universe to take care of the details for you. . . . You are stepping into the unknown with trust and belief that your life is just as you desire it to be. . . . Imagine your quantum self as a brilliant golden light that penetrates and is penetrated by everything that has ever been, is, or ever will be. . . . You are an intrinsic part of the Divine Plan . . . one facet of the cosmic web . . . an invaluable thread in the pattern of life. . . . Be aware of your potential . . . the potential that comes from your connection with all things in the universe. . . . Take a moment to enjoy that sense of energy . . . of no longer being bounded by a body . . . free from the limitations of your physical self.

(Pause for ten seconds.)

Move forwards now . . . towards the centre of the labyrinth where a special gift awaits you . . . a symbolic gift from your Higher Self. . . .

Close your eyes, if you have not already done so. . . . In your mind's eye see, in the centre of this special place, a small pool. . . . It is not gated or walled but open as it merges with the stones on the floor of the labyrinth. The water is still and very, very deep. Within this pool are kept many different objects with which seekers find the answer to whatever they are looking for. Imagine you are looking into the dark, shiny water and see your reflection staring back at you. . . . Feel your hand skim across the top of the water, letting the droplets trickle through your fingers. . . . The water is pleasantly warm. . . . It smells sweetly of flowers or herbs. . . . Now plunge your arm, your face or your whole body into the water – whichever you choose. . . . The pool is deep but safe, there is no current and you can come back to the surface any time you like. . . . There is an object, a symbol – something in the water that can help you with whatever challenge faces you at this moment. . . . This is the key to finding fulfilment in your life. . . . Go into the water now and bring it out.

(Pause for ten seconds.)

Look at your object. . . . Turn it round so you can see it from all angles. . . . Feel it, make a note of any colour. . . . Be clear about what it is but don't be concerned about what it means at this moment, unless you have an immediate insight. . . .

The Art of Non-attachment

The closer to our goal we travel, the more challenging – but more exciting and anticipatory – the journey appears to become. So it is with the two final labyrinthine pathways, which are concerned with the art of non-attachment and involve being open to the potential for new, unknown possibilities and living a destiny greater than you could have imagined for yourself.

Do you remember the story of King Canute? He was the son of a Danish invader of England and, after his father's death, was proclaimed king. Whether his head had been turned by the constant flattery of his courtiers or he was a born control freak, Canute got the idea that he was invincible even against the forces of nature. In order to prove his supremacy, legend has it that he sat on the banks of the River Trent at a time when the spring tides cause a high wall of water called the Aegir to rush upstream. Canute ordered the water not to wet him but was drenched regardless.

There is a little of Canute in all of us, especially those who constantly demand that the Universe gives us exactly what we want for our lives and thus try to manipulate and control everything that happens. But, king or commoner, we soon discover that nature cannot be mastered and that trying to control the unpredictability of life is an unnecessary waste of focus and energy. Never forget that destiny frequently has plans for us that far exceed our limited human imaginations.

Attachment to a specific outcome or set of outcomes is like shackling yourself to a partner – any partner – just because you don't trust that the ultimate relationship can be yours. Attachment is 'making do' based on fear thoughts. As a recovering control junkie, I know how hard it is to detach from what we *think* we want in order to live the life we are *meant* to have – to fulfil our true destiny.

Detachment is one of the hardest concepts to explain,

let alone embrace, yet it is vital that you do this from a heartfelt, emotional perspective and not from an intellectual one – which is why these pathways form the closing part of your journey. In a way, Morihei Ueshiba who is quoted at the start of this chapter is right – there really are few techniques that can help with this. This is the paradox: the noble quest for self-actualisation, fulfilment, enlightenment, or whatever you want to call it, is about non-action. By fervently trying to pursue and possess these states, your attachment to that achievement moves you further away from your goal. Now that you have articulated what you really want your life to be like and have taken steps to overcome the outmoded and dysfunctional habits that have anchored you to port rather than allowing you to sail to new shores, it is time to stop doing and just *be*.

Having said that, I believe that learning to detach from specific outcomes can be regarded as a skill and there is a four-step process to mastering it. The good news is that you have reached stage two already.

- Stage one is *unconscious incompetence* – you don't even realise you lack a particular ability or exhibit dysfunctional behaviour because you are so rooted in long-held habits. Simply by reading this book and engaging in the visualisations and exercises you will have begun to transcend that stage.

- Stage two is *conscious incompetence* – you may not yet have worked out how to accomplish this skill, but at least you know you want to change your life for the better.

- Stage three is *conscious competence* – you have emotionally and intellectually embraced the concept of change and are trying to put its various aspects into practice. However, you have to engage mentally each time: you have to *remember* to be skilful.

- Stage four is *unconscious competence* – you have

assimilated this understanding and it has now become second nature to you. Like an experienced driver, you no longer have to think about the various skills involved – you just use them. In terms of the goal that you have assigned yourself, you have stopped *doing* and have reached the ideal state of *being*.

Mental Manipulation

Some fascinating work being done at the Engineering Anomalies Research division at Princeton University in the US offers a scientific perspective on the spiritual law of detachment. One of the studies into the nature of human consciousness and its effects on the environment involved volunteers attempting to influence a sequence of machine-generated random numbers using only the power of their minds. The most successful results were achieved by those who, having made up their minds to achieve their goals, engaged in no further mental effort. In other words, they visualised what they wanted to achieve, took the appropriate action and then detached from the specific outcome – just letting it happen if it was meant to.

Those who were less successful were the ones who tried too hard, becoming mentally and physically frustrated by their inability to *force* the machine to do what they wanted it to. This is in line with what Deepak Chopra (acclaimed US guru whose writings blend Eastern wisdom and Western science) terms 'The Law of Least Effort', and the Taoist Way which espouses the paradox of 'Do without doing, Act without acting' that leads the wisest souls to 'get great things done'. Both allude to the idea that, because you are linking yourself harmoniously with the universe through following its laws, the path to total fulfilment becomes effortless and natural. It is like allowing the tide to sweep you forwards instead of trying to swim against it. It is about allowing the universe to take care of the details.

Detachment is more satisfying, a lot more fun and better for your mental and physical wellbeing than kidding yourself you are always in control. It has taken me a lifetime and a lot of painful experiences to come to this realisation, which is why I intend the explanations and exercises in this chapter to help you achieve this state of inner peace faster and more easily.

The World of Attachment

Let's start by looking at what you will be giving up when you reach this goal of freedom from the obsession with attachment. Frustration. Dissatisfaction. Unhappiness. Fear. Doubt. Pain. This may seem difficult to grasp at first, because we are all so conditioned to seeing the world through the filters of long-held beliefs, habits and attitudes. Yet we are blinkered almost from the day we are born because human beings only see what they want, expect or have learned to see. This is illustrated in the following story.

Joe, a record store owner, and Simon, a university lecturer, have gone on a camping trip together. On their first night they've had rather a lot to eat and drink and so fall soundly asleep. Suddenly, in the early hours of the morning, Joe wakes up and shakes his friend.

'Simon, look up and tell me what you see,' says Joe, still slightly the worse for wear.

Simon, a rather erudite individual, thinks about this for a moment and then replies, 'I see a beautiful star-filled sky.'

'And what does that tell you?' Joe persists.

'From a cosmological viewpoint it tells me that the universe has millions of galaxies with the potential for billions of planets, any one of which might harbour many different life forms. In terms of my faith in a Higher Power I recognise that humankind is but a small and insignificant part of God's overall plan. Astrologically I notice that Mars is conjunct Venus. From the faint light coming up from the east I deduce it's around five-thirty. And weather-wise I think we're going to see a fine day. Why, what does it tell you?'

Joe raises his eyes in exasperation and blurts out: 'That someone has come along and stolen our tent, you fool!'

In my workshops I use a number of different games and exercises which have been devised by psychologists to demonstrate that how we perceive things may be quite different from the way our colleagues, family or partner see them. If you have ever attended a personal development workshop which explores the nature of perception, you may have been shown a picture which appeared in the *American Journal of Psychiatry* in 1930 as part of an article entitled: 'A New Ambiguous Figure'. It is a drawing of a female figure that can be perceived either as the side view of an attractive, well-dressed and obviously wealthy young woman, or as a hook-nosed, sharp-chinned old hag. Another picture, devised by a psychologist at the State University of New York in Buffalo, looks at first like a black and white photograph of an unidentifiable landmass with a series of offshore islands. Some people do not realise it is actually a picture of a calf's head until it is pointed out to them.

As human beings we constantly place limitations on ourselves and fail to expand our capacity to create alternative solutions to life's challenges because we relate to new experiences only in the context of the past. As untold spiritual teachers have told, enlightenment – having greater clarity of perception – is only achieved by freshly experiencing life moment by moment. Like the hero's journey or venturing into the labyrinth, we cannot know what lies ahead of us, only trust that we have the inner resources to overcome anything we are faced with. The calmer, more centred and more harmoniously attuned to the universe we are through detaching ourselves from specific outcomes, the easier it is to trust that our lives are meant to be glorious and fulfilling. But, like the chicken and egg conundrum, it is impossible to state which comes first.

Mind Tricks

In the same way that the police are often hampered by the fact that witnesses to the same crime frequently offer different 'facts' – such as the colour of a car involved in a hit-and-run accident, for example – each of us may be imprisoning ourselves in a victim mentality by focusing on memories that are not entirely accurate.

CASE HISTORY: Jerry's Story

Jerry's adult life was being detrimentally affected by the abuse which he perceived had been heaped upon him as a young child by his parents. Sackings, redundancy, two divorces and estrangement from his children had pushed Jerry to the edge of his ability to cope. Frightened and confused, he felt under siege and began to blame his parents for 'destroying his life'.

A frequent bed-wetter as a youngster, Jerry recalled in therapy how when he was only four or five years old his mother had locked him in a shed along with the family dog to 'teach him a lesson'. Jerry's perception of his childhood was an unhappy one and, ironically, throughout his adult life he had played out a pattern of victimhood in which he regarded himself as being mentally, emotionally and even physically abused by those people he allowed to get close to him.

While working with his labyrinth pathways, Jerry was inspired to challenge this perception of reality and decided to speak to his parents and siblings about his memories. He reasoned that if the events he described had indeed happened he could then discuss the different attitude towards parenting which he held from his mother and father and, in understanding where they were 'coming from' at the time, perhaps forgive actions that had taken place over forty years previously.

With great courage, Jerry arranged to discuss these painful memories with his elderly parents in a non-confrontational way. His mother denied ever having locked her son outdoors overnight or any other abuses, but admitted that in her exasperation she had *threatened* to do so on several occasions. Jerry was confused by the fact that his parents were obviously upset at being told of these memories. After a long discussion he accepted that over time his mind had turned these threats into actual events, and he had thereby allowed his imagination to fuel a lifelong perception of himself as a victim.

This discovery proved to be immensely powerful and liberating to Jerry. Once he had learned to reframe his view of himself as no longer a victim of life, Jerry found it easier to accept responsibility for what happened to him and both his professional and personal life – once seemingly in tatters – was rebuilt.

What Jerry's story highlights is that our mind can play very cruel tricks on us, filtering all experiences according to an old life script or label we have attached to ourselves. Once your thoughts about yourself change, then your life changes – including your past. Jerry had the potential for a joyful, fulfilling life just as each one of us has. He just had to detach himself from his outmoded, dysfunctional attitude of 'victim'.

Spaced Out

Even in outer space there is no such thing as 'nothingness'. Cosmologists are discovering that what was once considered 'empty space' is actually a quantum soup of 'virtual' particles whose existence cannot be directly detected. Now take a look at this page. Study it carefully. It consists of black printed words on a white background. But which gives you the opportunity to perceive those words – the print or the white space? Surely it is both – if there were nothing but words on this page you would be presented with a mass of indecipherable black print. The white or empty space is what allows you to gain a sense of meaning from the whole. This means that the white 'void' is not empty but full of potential.

Similarly, space in our lives is invaluable for ascribing a

sense of purpose and meaning to our existence. Not only that, but it offers the opportunity to perceive something that previously we may not have recognised and is a stimulus for discerning a plethora of creative solutions. You are now being invited to increase the amount of 'white space' in your life, and the exercises in the rest of this chapter will help you achieve this.

For many of us, present-moment awareness is an enormous challenge. Either our minds are embroiled in the past, reviewing things we wish we had done differently or saying things we had failed to say but are now eating us up; or we are living in the future, planning – often like a military campaign – all the things we intend to do or say for a set of circumstances that may never actually happen. Yet the present is the only reality we have. The only value of the past is to offer us lessons from which we can learn to do things differently in the present; whereas the future is best regarded as being created from the actions and attitudes we display in the present. Why waste your time and energy on regrets for the past and fears for the future (which may never come to anything) when there is so much to enjoy in the moment? This is why the focus of spiritual teachers has always been on living for today and making every second as glorious as possible.

This exercise will help you discover where your past, present and future lie. It is adapted from an NLP technique called time lines.

Detach Exercise 1: The Path to Fulfilment

Find a comfortable place where you won't be disturbed for a little while and close your eyes. Think about something that has happened in your past – such as where you were last Christmas or how you spent your summer holiday. What is the mental direction from which that memory came? If it was from behind you, that is a healthy place for your past to be – unless it is attached to you in some way, like a backpack or cloak. However, if this memory appeared to come from in front of you then the only way you can get to your future is through your past, and therefore you will persistently repeat past behaviours. If the memory appeared to come from either side of you, there is still some degree in which past experiences are likely to inform present ones.

Now imagine there is a line of time that runs through you, with your past behind you, the present where you are standing and the future in front of you. This may take the form of a road, a border or a line of some sort – choose whatever is most appealing to you. My time line is the yellow brick road that I remember from the Judy Garland film The Wizard of Oz.

Recall the past memory you have just conjured up and, in your imagination, pivot it so that it is now positioned behind you on your time line, at an appropriate distance. Be aware of any uncomfortable physical or mental sensations that occur as you do this. Now turn your back on this past memory and look to your future. Conjure up whatever image seems appropriate. You may feel more comfortable seeing your future as a road extending far into the distance. Or perhaps your future may be over the brow of a hill or the horizon, so that its secrets are not accessible until you move forward from the present. Fix this visualisation in your mind's eye: your past firmly positioned behind you on your time line where you stand in the present, and the future up ahead of you. Fully experience this image.

There are several benefits from this time line exercise other than ensuring that past, present and future are appropriately positioned in your mind. First, you can use this technique to work through challenging or risky new behaviours by stepping on to your time line in your imagination and 'jumping' forward into the future. From this vantage point you can not only look back to see how you safely and successfully overcame your problems, but you can motivate yourself in the present by enjoying having eliminated them. This shift in perspective will help you make the changes necessary for a more fulfilled life.

Another benefit which I have used constantly in my desire to overcome relationship challenges is to ensure that all former lovers are securely positioned behind me on my time line. In order to 'see' them I have to look over my shoulder. Because they are in my past, I no longer allow them to encroach on my current or future life. This ensures that, while learning from my previous unsatisfactory choices and mistakes, I don't allow these men to inform my future. Just by visualising them behind me I speed up the time it takes me to get over an unhappy love affair.

However, don't be misled into regarding this as a one-off, 'quick fix' technique. Your success depends on your determination to position the past firmly behind you on an ongoing basis, because it tends to creep up on you unexpectedly in an attempt to keep events and situations in the forefront of your mind. Whenever you find something from your former life occupying an inappropriate position in your present or future, don't be afraid to consign it back where it belongs – in your past.

Repeating the above visualisation exercise on a regular basis will help you fix yourself firmly in the present, with all the attendant benefits which that state offers. In Chapter 3 you did an exercise in present-moment awareness (p. 70) which, repeated regularly, will help you become more attuned to the present and therefore detached from past and future regrets and fears. This awareness, also known as mindfulness, or Vipassana meditation, plays an important part in Buddhism and is a daily form of meditation that can be practised anywhere at any time. The Vipassana method requires paying attention to all physical movements and activities, emotions and other mental states or concepts. Here is a fun, creative exercise I have devised to help you achieve mindfulness.

Detach Exercise 2: Alien Encounters

Imagine that for one day only you have agreed to let an alien being take over your body, so that it can report objectively back to its own species on what it is like to be human. Once the alien takes you over you still remember everything about your life but have no vested interest in whatever happens to you over the course of that day – you simply observe objectively. The alien is privy to your feelings and emotions and everything that goes on in your head, but is separate from them in a way that, as a human, you might find difficult.

As this objective alien observer, be aware of what happens during this day as you detach yourself from events and sensations. When you feel an emotion, label it as 'confusion', 'sadness', 'joy' or whatever. Be aware of what that sensation is like and how it differs from others you may have experienced. In this attentive, non-attached state you may notice subtle nuances of behaviour in yourself and others that you may have missed before. Note what these are, either mentally or by writing them in your journal, so that you can reflect on them later.

Once you have completed your alien experience, it's time to consider what you have learned from it:

- How was this day different?
- How did that feel?
- What did you enjoy about this experience and what were the benefits?
- To what extent were you able to discern the difference between, and accurately name, emotional states – both yours and other people's?
- How far do you allow your thoughts and behaviours to be dependent on certain conditions in your life?
- If you were to change these conditions, to what extent would you be able to eliminate certain negative/dysfunctional thoughts and behaviours?

- Given what you have learned about yourself and others from this exercise, what do you intend to do differently in future?

- In what circumstances might it be useful to revisit this exercise in future?

Emotional Intelligence

The above exercise, in which you are encouraged to become more aware of the different facets of your emotions, those of others and the way in which these interplay, is an important part of what is called Emotional Intelligence (EQ). This concept came into prominence in management in 1996 with the publication of Daniel Goleman's best-selling book of the same name. He stated that success at work is 80 per cent dependent on emotional intelligence, with IQ contributing only 20 per cent to that success. High EQ individuals are more self-aware, which gives them the ability to manage their own emotions more effectively as well as enhancing their empathy and handling of other people. In a world in which interpersonal skills are recognised as playing an increasingly important role in the workplace, enhancing your EQ not only ensures greater personal fulfilment because of your success in dealing with yourself and others, but boosts your employability. A piece of 1980s research conducted by the Center for Creative Leadership in Greensboro, North Carolina in the US, one of the largest institutions working to generate and disseminate knowledge about leadership and its development, backs this up. It found that a key factor in whether highly intelligent and technically skilled individuals reached the top of their organisations or not was the manager's ability to handle their own, and other people's, emotions. Skills, qualifications and experience are not the only factors on the road to career success, and that will undoubtedly continue to be the case as we journey through a more emotionally focused millennium.

Detach Exercise 3: What If?

This short exercise allows you quickly to reframe experiences whenever you find yourself getting mentally enmeshed in past mistakes or future fears. Whatever is happening to you right now, ask yourself this question: 'What if this were all all right?' Then repeat the following affirmation to yourself: 'Everything is unfolding as it should.' Accompanied by some deep breathing and relaxation, this is a wonderful, instant way to overcome the discomfort of living anywhere other than in the present.

Detach Exercise 4: The Labyrinthine Gift

At the centre of your labyrinth you intuited a special gift – a symbolic message from your Higher Self that offers further insights into finding fulfilment in whatever form is most meaningful for you. Without turning this book into an encyclopaedia of symbols and trying to suggest what significance they may have in your life – which is neither practical nor advisable – here are some general guidelines on excavating the meaning of this particular message, together with examples of how some of my clients have used these guidelines to discern the unique communication from their Higher Selves. Remember, as an essential part of the universal matrix you have access to all past, present and future knowledge. Although certain common symbolic themes are threaded through the lives of otherwise quite separate and different people, no one except you can really know or understand the sacred purpose of this gift.

1. In your journal, draw or fully describe the symbolic gift from the pool at the centre of your labyrinth so that its characteristics don't become lost in your memory.
2. Research everything you can about this symbol across a wide range of subjects from its history to its religious significance.
3. Check the derivation of the name of this symbol in a

dictionary and look to see what other concepts are associated with it.

4. Ask your Higher Self for help in uncovering what this message means. Then be alert to the language of symbols as expressed through dreams, coincidences, animal totems and insights. If necessary, explore techniques used by native and contemporary pagans and shamans to understand the clues connecting us with the Divine through nature.

5. Work on enhancing your intuition (see pp. 115–126) so that when you receive appropriate hunches you will recognise them and act on them.

6. Above all, trust that what you need to know will come to you in keeping with your new-found belief that everything is unfolding as it should.

CASE HISTORY: Sandra's Story

Sandra had never found her work as a top secretary/PA to be particularly satisfying. Despite having career counselling and taking various occupational tests, she still couldn't track down a job she felt passionate about. This was having a knock-on effect on her health. Underpinned by the gnawing sense that she should be doing something more meaningful with her life, Sandra found her high-pressure role very stressful and this resulted in frequent migraines and back problems.

Her labyrinthine symbol was a *child's rattle*. Although they had been married for four years, Sandra and her husband had decided to put off having children until they were more financially secure. However, this symbolic message caused Sandra to reassess her priorities. A year later she had her first baby, a little girl they called Chloe, and told her company that she would not be returning to work. As a full-time wife, mother and homemaker Sandra found that she was making so many savings on their previous lifestyle – from the cost of commuting into London to convenience shopping – that the loss of her salary hadn't affected their standard of living at all. More importantly, Sandra has discovered that the personal fulfilment of having a child far outweighs any professional success she might have achieved.

CASE HISTORY: Charles's Story

When Charles pulled a *leather-bound book* from the waters of his labyrinthine pool, he discovered that its pages were blank. Having intuited that this was an instruction manual for his life, he was perplexed and not a little concerned about what this 'empty' message meant. Charles agreed to meditate on his symbol over the coming weeks, as well as work on the concept of non-attachment from the final labyrinthine pathways which he had sensed contained the most important lessons for him. After practising Vipassana or mindfulness meditation for several months, Charles discovered that when he revisited the image of this book it had begun to be filled with the most beautiful copperplate writing and illustrations. He felt this indicated that living purposefully in the present, and not getting caught up with a lifelong obsession with the past and particularly the future, was filling his life (the book) with knowledge and thus power. Charles recognised that his previous task-oriented mode of existence was an empty way of living his life, and as page after page became gloriously filled he was further motivated towards embracing present-moment awareness.

CASE HISTORY: James's Story

James's labyrinthine symbol was a *Tibetan singing bowl* that he said made the most beautiful, harmonious sound. He had been a gifted musician as a young man but over the years this aspect of his life had been sacrificed to his City job, particularly to meet the financial requirements of his ambitious wife. James recognised that a vital part of him had died when he started to ignore his love of music and so he began to set aside a few hours a week – then a whole morning, then a complete Sunday – to indulge his passion. As this outlet began to fire him up, James began to feel and even look different. He suddenly rediscovered his zest for life as a whole, not just for his music, and found that he could accomplish work in a much shorter space of time because he felt so energised. His wife, rather than being alienated as a result, began to look at James with fresh eyes, too. Having relit a spark that had lain dormant within him for over two decades, he found their love life was improving. Now, when James gets back from the various global music festivals he travels to alone (by mutual choice), he says he feels excited at the prospect of coming home to his wife – something he thought could not be possible after so many years of apathetic marriage.

CASE HISTORY: Freya's Story

Freya pulled out a *diamond-studded cross* from her laybrinthine pool. She was puzzled by the overtly religious connotation, having been a lapsed Catholic since early adulthood, and immediately rejected any notion of reclaiming her faith. Instead of focusing too much on this part of the symbolism, Freya decided to research all she could about diamonds. In one book she discovered that a diamond – the hardest-known natural mineral – is made from the same element as graphite, the soft 'lead' in pencils. The difference is simply that, while diamonds have a rigid, compact atomic structure, the carbon in graphite lies in weakly bonded, sheet-like layers that are widely spaced. In crystal healing, diamonds are used to cure nightmares (imagined fears!); Napoleon used to have one on his sword scabbard, which he believed made him invincible.

To Freya there was an analogy with her attitude towards religion. While she felt that Catholicism was too rigid a philosophy for her to follow, she recognised that without some form of spiritual expression her life was missing a vital element that gave purpose and meaning, thereby helping her overcome certain fears. She began to explore alternative practices and, uncomfortable with those that had set rules and rituals, decided to embrace Buddhism as a way of living her life with respect and care for the human race as well as for all the other species on the planet. Through this Buddhist approach, Freya found a sense of peace and connectedness that had hitherto been missing from her life.

Ever Onwards. . . .

Our journey together is not yet over. There is still the return out of the labyrinth to experience. In Chapter 7 we shall explore ways in which this journey of personal change can be reinforced.

7

THE RETURN

The end of all our exploring
Will be to arrive at where we started
And to know the place for the first time.

T. S. Eliot, 'Little Gidding', Four Quartets

The Labyrinth Visualisation *Part 4*

Now it's time to come out of the labyrinth. Place the object back into the water for someone else to find. . . . And open your eyes. . . .

You now have all the treasure you need to lead a life of self-fulfilment, to become complete and whole and fulfil your life's mission. . . . As you retrace your steps through the labyrinth, in silence, and with the pathways imprinted in your mind's eye, think about all the gifts you have been offered. . . . Consider the connection between them . . . what pattern they suggest. . . . How you might use them to best effect in your life. . . . In a moment there will be only the names and numbers of the pathways in reverse order, followed by silence or gentle background music as you make your way out of your labyrinth . . . the single road that led you in . . . as it will lead you out. . . . Take your time over this final part of the process. . . . Leave the centre of your labyrinth now and move into. . . .

Pathway 7 – where you discovered your energetic Self, the Self that is without physical form and hence boundaries. . . .

(Pause.)

Pathway 6 – where you came upon your mystery mentor . . . someone whose life will act as a constant source of inspiration and wisdom. . . .

(Pause.)

Pathway 5 – where you received the gift of intuition, the flashes of inspiration that are always available to you and which represent your innate homing device for success. . . .

(Pause.)

Pathway 4 – in which you committed to one specific change in your behaviour and hence to redirect the course of your life. . . .

(Pause.)

Pathway 3 – where you considered all the little details of the changes that you will implement to make your future life even more of a reality. . . .

(Pause.)

Pathway 2 – where you acutely sensed the tension between the life you have and the life you are meant to lead. . . .

(Pause.)

And Pathway 1 – the video showing what your life will be like if you continue on the path you are travelling now. . . .

(Pause.)

Now you have reached the mouth of your imaginary labyrinth.. . . Take a moment to become aware of the room which you are currently in . . . open your eyes, if they are closed, stretch your arms and legs . . . take a drink or light snack and gradually re-orient yourself.

Congratulations. . . . The first part of your journey is over. . . . Now it's time to work with the insights offered to you by your Higher Self . . . and to learn how to use them in your life so that every day is as fulfilling, enthusiastic and centred as you would like it to be.

Emerging from the labyrinth signals not the end of your journey, but the beginning. Like sitting on a remote mountain to meditate or going on a silent retreat, it is not so much the insights you gain during your spiritual pilgrimage that are important but what you do with them; in particular, how you integrate this new way of thinking, working and being into your everyday life.

This final chapter continues the themes of Dream, Do and Detach that weave their way through this book. However, this time they come in a slightly different order. I want to leave you with additional practical tools and techniques and motivational knowledge with which to fuel your desire for personal change and finding fulfilment.

After briefly looking at the various processes that underpin human action and experience, we will explore together what you can *Do* to overcome physical and mental apathy; how to use emotionally empowered *Dreams* to over-ride even the most deep-seated negative beliefs and then *Detach* yourself from the desire for total change; to accept that there are some challenging aspects of your life which are essential to your future growth and personal/spiritual development as well as the 'shadow' characteristics that complete the whole of your Self.

Three Sets of Influences

While one person can give up smoking 'just like that', others may need various methods from nicotine patches to a course of hypnotherapy to help them conquer their addiction. And sometimes even the most strong-willed and self-aware individuals can feel overpowered on days when both your physical body and conscious mind seem to be conspiring to sabotage the dreams of your Higher Self.

The Head of Psychology at the UK's Open University, Dr

Richard Stevens, has identified three kinds of processes which underpin human action and experience. He has called his model Trimodal Theory, and its value lies in helping us understand how each of these modes might affect us so that we can use this knowledge to bring about long-lasting and effective change. Stevens's three processes are:

The Primary or Biological Mode

This mode describes our individual biochemical, psychophysical and genetic inheritances such as temperament, predisposition to certain diseases and aptitudes as well as action patterns specific to humans as a species, such as sexual styles, altruism and responses to authority.

The Secondary or Symbolic Mode

This mode describes the way in which our individual behaviours, attitudes and the sense of meaning we ascribe to our experiences have been shaped by our cultural history, including our ethnic background and parental upbringing.

The Tertiary or Reflexive Mode

This mode describes our capacity for self-awareness and the extent to which we use this innate ability to self-monitor and imagine more empowering alternatives for our lives.

The Mind–Body Link

While the previous chapters dealt largely with reflexivity and symbolism, it is important that we also focus on the Primary level of Dr Stevens's model. While orthodox approaches assume a deterministic stance – that we are 'stuck with' our biology, having little or no control over our biochemical processes – experience shows that this is not strictly accurate. Indeed, we are socially encouraged to control certain bodily functions the moment our primary carers decide it's time for 'potty training'. Some child development 'experts' have even

suggested that parents regulate their child's eating and defe-
cation patterns to confirm to a rigid timetable.

We have already seen how a technique known as
biofeedback (see p. 67) can help people consciously alter
their rate of heartbeat and even body temperature. With
sufficient practice and motivation, some exceptional individuals have learned to control various bodily functions
without the use of the electronic instruments that usually
support this form of relaxation training.

It is known that deep relaxation changes the level of
arousal of the brain's limbic circuitry – the part of the brain
associated with emotions – which in turn affects the body's
production of certain chemicals such as adrenalin. It also
influences instinctive drives such as the need for food or
sex, which is why prolonged periods of intense relaxation
have been found to facilitate fasting and sexual abstinence.
Some people, fired up by a belief or cause for which they
are prepared to die, can even overcome the body's instinctive need for food and drink. Even at a basic biochemical
level, our bodies can be controlled by what goes on in our
minds. This was borne out in a psychological experiment
conducted a number of years ago in which a group of
elderly men were 'transported' back to the days of their
youth. They spent a week in an environment that re-created
the life they would have led in their thirties and forties,
even down to reading newspapers from that time and
eating different foods from their current diets. They wore
the fashions of the day and listened to the music of that
period. What the psychologists found was that the particip-
ants began to act and even look years younger.
Additionally, their mental faculties improved. It was as if,
having engrossed themselves in a life of many decades
earlier, their physical bodies followed suit.

In her ground-breaking book *Molecules of Emotion*, US
neuroscientist Candace Pert describes how she established
the biomolecular basis of emotions and put the mind–body
link firmly in the scientific domain and not just in the realm

of metaphysics. And a special issue of *Scientific American* in 1997, headlined 'Mysteries of the Mind', devoted eight pages to an article on the continuous signals that take place between the brain and the immune system and on a discussion of how our state of mind influences our health.

During my workshops I use two visualisation techniques to demonstrate this mind–body link. The first involves asking you to recall a pleasurable experience or incident, such as the face of a loved one, your wedding day or the moment when your child spoke his or her first word. When you do this you usually find yourself smiling spontaneously. You *think* happy thoughts and your body responds with a joyous expression.

The second visualisation involves thinking vividly of a lemon. After employing all the senses to make this experience seem as real as possible – even down to the way it feels to dig your nails into the waxy skin and watch the juice oozing out over your hands – your mouth gets a boost of saliva, just as it would if you were actually breaking open a lemon. So the message is that you do have more influence over what happens to your physical body than you may have given yourself credit for.

However, there are days when frankly you just don't feel all that great. Perhaps you're depressed, your energy levels are low and, rather than focus on all the never-ending objectives and tasks involved in achieving that golden vision for your life, you just want to give up and go back to bed. We're not talking acute depression, here, where medical intervention may be required to regulate the biochemistry of the brain, but the sort of lethargy-inducing, motivation-zapping 'blues' that all of us suffer from occasionally. At such times you may need to employ some of the following techniques to put you back in control of what is happening to you psychophysically.

Change That Pattern

1. Investigate how your diet and general lifestyle may be

contributing to your see-saw moods. Dose up on vitamin and mineral supplements by all means, but don't ignore the detrimental effect of a high-fat, sugar-rich, processed and junk-food diet washed down with too much tea, coffee and alcohol on your mental as well as your physical health. No longer seen as 'quackery', nutritional therapy from both orthodox and alternative medical practitioners is being found to prevent and reverse various forms of mental illness and degenerative conditions including Alzheimer's disease, depression, schizophrenia, memory loss and insomnia, as well as general tiredness and irritability. There are a number of leading experts in this field but I can highly recommend books by health guru Leslie Kenton, Patrick Holford of the UK's Institute for Optimum Nutrition, and Dr Michael Colgan of the Colgan Institute of Nutritional Science in San Diego, USA.

2. Find a 'subtle energy' health maintenance system that works for you. Energetically, your physical body is susceptible to blockages that, even if they don't result in a disease you can put a name to, will cause you to feel 'under par', 'not firing on all cylinders' or 'tired all the time'. Alternative therapies such as acupuncture, acupressure, polarity therapy and energy healing, that work on the chakra system to rebalance the flow of life force known in the East as *chi* or *prana*, can help enhance your mental, physical and emotional wellbeing.

3. Find an exercise programme that you will be motivated to stick at. Aerobic fitness regimes have been shown to reduce the memory, cognitive and hormonal decline that we associate with ageing. In 1991 the *American Journal of Epidemiology* published a study of six thousand US citizens which found that those who engaged in some form of physical activity had a much lower risk of depression than those who were inactive. In another short piece of US research, students engaging in a single bout of exercise significantly reduced their levels of

anger and anxiety. However, it is important to indulge only in exercise that you enjoy, as UK sports psychologists have recently discovered that forcing yourself to take part in sports or other physical activities which you do not like impairs your overall wellbeing more than not taking any exercise at all.

4. Look for ways in which you can enhance the amount and quality of sleep that you get each night. In addition to getting to the root cause of an overstimulated nervous system, stress and anxiety through nutrition and physical exercise, there are a number of other techniques that can help. These include homeopathic remedies and/or tissue salts, herbal teas and/or pillows, water therapy, aromatherapy oils, breathing and visualisation exercises. One old wives' remedy that has always worked for me is to dissolve a tablespoon of good-quality honey in a glass of pure grape juice. A lifelong insomniac, I am usually nodding off within twenty minutes of drinking that concoction. I have no idea why, but who cares when I get the effect I want?

5. Through the previous exercises outlined in this book such as Alien Encounters (on p. 139) you will have become increasingly aware of even subtle changes in your moods and will be able to name them accurately. This enhancement of your Emotional Intelligence means that whenever you sense an attack of negativity or depression coming on you will be in a better position to do something to interrupt that process in a positive way. Try the following ideas:

- Put on some of your favourite dance music and imagine you are Patrick Swayze's partner in his latest film.

- Be aware of your posture and take on the demeanour of a positive person by casting your eyes upwards instead of down, straightening your back, and holding your head up high.

- Go out for a brisk walk and fully connect with as

much of nature as is available to you – even if it's just observing the way the birds fly.

- Play a silly game, ideally with others but by yourself if necessary. Recall some of the games you played as a child – hopscotch, marbles, dressing up – and indulge yourself in some fun for a change.

- Challenge yourself to finish a word puzzle or cross-word within a certain time – and focus on that problem instead of the ones in your head.

- Smile and laugh, even if you don't feel you have anything humorous to focus on. The physical act of smiling releases endorphins, the brain chemicals that induce a natural 'high' during prolonged bouts of exercise. Since laughter is infectious, buy or borrow a recording of someone laughing – or make a tape of your own for such circumstances – and within moments you'll be suffusing your body with natural opiates.

- Talk to your negative self. Whenever I am feeling less than 100 per cent, I say out loud: 'Oh, it's just Liz getting depressed/negative/silly/irrational. Come on, girl, stop being so self-indulgent.' And then I imagine I am coaxing that part of myself to get involved with something to take my mind off my problems.

- Likewise, when you feel a downward spiral coming on, just say 'Stop!' and mentally refuse to let that negative thought take hold. Again, try to do something physically or mentally engrossing that will help you focus on something other than your mood.

- Read some positive affirmations.

- Inspire yourself by creating a Personal Passions Poster. Take a large sheet of thin card and glue on to it whatever you can find in books, magazines or catalogues – colours, shapes, faces, key words and so on that relate to your golden vision – to provide yourself with instant motivational feedback whenever you feel low.

A Mind Once Stretched. . . .

. . . by a new idea is changed for ever. So says one of the inspirational posters which I am fond of buying to decorate my home. There are many historical examples that bear this out. For example, despite the fact that the first manned space flight, by the USSR, had taken place only a month earlier, on 25 May 1961 US President John F. Kennedy announced that the Americans would put a man on the moon before the end of the decade. The US space programme was nowhere near so advanced at the time, but it has been suggested that it was this very public declaration which stretched and inspired the minds of the American public as well as those of the men and women working on the space programme. As personal development guru Dr Wayne Dyer is fond of saying, 'When you believe it, you'll see it' (as opposed to the doubting Thomas mode we normally get locked into). And, indeed, the first men to walk on the moon were Americans Neil Armstrong and Buzz Aldrin on 21 July 1969. President Kennedy's assertion had become reality.

Similarly, no athlete had run a mile in less than four minutes before the UK's Roger Bannister did so in 1954. The following year, scores of other runners had equalled that time; the year after, hundreds of athletes had. And world champion boxer Mohammed Ali was telling everyone he was the greatest long before he actually was. Beliefs are constructions, and as such we can change them any time we choose. It is simply a case of focusing your mind on positives and benefits rather than on the opposite. Admittedly this is easier said than done, but if you regard this as a skill just like any other you can see how moving from unconscious incompetence to unconscious competence simply involves thought and continual practice.

One of the most inspiring examples of someone who did this innately was the prolific inventor Thomas Edison – a man, incidentally, whom teachers had labelled as having an 'addled brain' and whose father considered him stupid. The fact that Edison had only had three months of formal schooling by the age of eight was probably a strong contributor to his retaining his innate creativity. By the end of his life Edison held some 1300 patents, the equivalent of one innovation every three weeks. Like all creative geniuses, he had many 'failures'. However, rather than considering them as such, he regarded each flop as moving him closer and closer towards success. As he put it himself, 'I am not disheartened, because every wrong attempt discarded is another step forward.' Thanks to this remarkable man's persistence and self-belief humankind was blessed with the filament light bulb, the microphone and the gramophone as well as hundreds of other devices. What is the world missing out on because *you* choose to stop trying?

Personal Choice

You can manipulate and control where you put your attention, and deliberately choose a positive frame for your thoughts, just as history's most successful and inspiring figures have done. It's up to you. Becoming aware of a tendency to look on the downside of things and deciding to do it differently moves you into the realm of conscious competence before you become an unconsciously optimistic person. This is an area in which I believe a spiritual perspective is invaluable. My own and my clients' experiences have demonstrated that belief in a purposeful, loving universe helps put problems in perspective. They are no longer the insurmountable obstacles of the spiritually redundant, but a means of assisting us to grow and develop beyond our wildest imaginations. Don't just take my word for it – read what the following inspirational teachers have had to say about living in perfect harmony with the universe:

> *The moment one definitely commits oneself, then Providence moves too.*
> Johann Wolfgang von Goethe (1749–1832),
> German writer and polymath

No pessimist ever discovered the secrets of the stars, or sailed to an uncharted land, or opened a new heaven to the human spirit.
Helen Keller (1880–1968), US essayist, author and counsellor on international relations for the American Foundation for the Blind

Suffering ceases to be suffering at the moment it finds a meaning, such as the meaning of a sacrifice.
Viktor E. Frankl (1905–1997), renowned Austrian psychiatrist and Holocaust survivor

A man who suffers before it is necessary, suffers more than is necessary.
Seneca (4 BC–AD 65), Roman philosopher and playwright

Assumption-busting

So, how are you getting on with changing your beliefs about yourself and the nature of life itself? How easy are you finding it to reframe your experiences in a more positive way? If you are still challenged by this, let me outline a psychological technique called attribution theory which may help you understand how self-motivated, successful, fulfilled individuals think, so you can model that should you wish to do so. It concerns the underlying assumptions that we make about ourselves and our ability to control external events.

Imagine two colleagues named Jane and John, with comparable IQs and work experience, who are doing the same job in different organisations. Janet is a high achiever with a prolific output who never seems to suffer from stress, whereas John finds his work extremely challenging and finds it difficult to shake off long bouts of depression. Aside from their different levels of material success, Jane considers life to be much more joyous and rewarding than John. Here's why.

Both Jane and John are asked to apply for a more senior position in their respective organisations. Neither gets the job. When asked by her partner how she feels about this, Jane admits she's disappointed and says it was obvious that there was a more experienced or skilled candidate and perhaps she didn't prepare herself as well as she might. Once she knows who the successful person is she intends to compare that person's skills, qualifications and interpersonal traits with her own to try and plug some of the gaps. Because she wants promotion, Jane is committed to finding out what she can do differently next time. She believes that while she was unlucky on this occasion, the right opportunity will present itself in the future – and next time she will be ready to exploit it. Now motivated to do this, Jane puts the experience behind her and gets on with her life.

John, on the other hand, is all doom and gloom when his partner asks him about the promotion. He believes that his failure to meet various targets in the past has counted against him and that this lack of success is all his fault for being generally hopeless. John has got it into his head that he has never really fitted in at his place of work and that his bosses are trying to get rid of him. Since he is convinced that there is nothing he can do to change this situation, John decides to avoid the indignity of failure in the future by not applying for any more promotions. To his mind, he has no chance of progressing in the company and this makes him feel demotivated and lethargic.

The difference between Jane's beliefs or attributions and John's can be summed up as follows:

- Jane externalised the experience, while John personalised it, believing that he didn't get the promotion because he was 'useless.'

- Jane believed this was a one-off blip in her career progression which she could do something about, while John regarded it as the sort of insurmountable obstacle that was always placed before him.

- Jane knows that sometimes life doesn't give you what you want precisely when you want it, but that it's not a persistent theme in her life. John, on the other hand, believes his difficulties will continue in all areas of his life.

You can see how these two individuals have set up very different self-fulfilling prophecies.

What attribution theory suggests is that positive thinkers regard unfortunate experiences as being situational, local and unstable. Those who succumb to a state of mind called 'learned helplessness' regard them as personal (their fault), pervasive (happen to them in all circumstances) and permanent (will keep happening).

Now think of a recent situation when you were disappointed at the outcome, and review your thinking according to these factors. Assumptions are anathema to creative thinkers because they shackle you to one set of often outworn beliefs and behaviours. They are also the antithesis of self-knowledge.

EXERCISE: Testing your Assumption-making Habits

You are the parent of two little girls, who have come into the kitchen each needing a lemon. However, you only have one left. What options are available to you?

When I introduce this puzzle to my workshop clients, typical responses include:

- Going to the shops to buy another lemon.
- Tossing a coin to see which child gets the lemon.
- Cutting the lemon in half and asking each child to make do with that.
- Telling them you're not going to have them fighting over a lemon so they can forget about it.

In fact, the first thing to do would be to ask the girls what they wanted to use the lemon for. Having found that one wanted a little bit of zest to put in the icing of a cake and the other wanted the juice for a drink, there is not an issue since they can share the lemon.

Remember what I wrote earlier about asking questions rather than seeking solutions? If you continually stop and question why you are thinking or behaving in a certain way and can recognise that you may be succumbing to old patterns, then you have the space in which to make considered changes to the way you live your life.

Reinforcing Tactics

Not long ago I decided to take up salsa dancing. I enjoyed this new form of fun and exercise very much and picked up the basic steps quite easily. Unfortunately, a series of trips and meetings meant that after a few weeks I had to stop going to the weekly class. Before long I had forgotten all I had learned. Similarly, the insights you have gained from your journey into the labyrinth will only stay with you if you reinforce them regularly. As a great admirer of Dr Deepak Chopra's *The Seven Spiritual Laws of Success* I would like to suggest that you take each of the themes of the labyrinth pathways and integrate them into your life on a daily or weekly basis, as his book does. Here are some examples of what you could do:

Vision

- Make this the day when you take special notice of your dreams and record them in a dream journal.

- Revisit your futurelife chart (see p. 87) and create a visual like the Personal Passions Poster (see p. 154) to illustrate one or more of your visionary goals.

- Recall one compelling visionary image from Pathway 1 and imbue this with as much emotion as you can. Really see, feel, smell, touch and taste this creative image, so that you become physiologically as well as mentally excited by it.

- Check if there are any further life areas you want to add to your futurelife chart.

- Daydream about the future screenplay for your life from Pathway 1. As you do so, play at making the image bigger, brighter, more colourful, more animated and with a soundtrack.

Tension

- Be aware today of the differences between where you are and where you want to be. Then commit to moving out of your comfort zone.

- Where the loss of your old habits/behaviours/attitudes/life is concerned, become consciously aware of what part of the grieving process (see p. 90) you are currently in.

- Be more conscious of the choices and decisions you are making today and how they will affect your future. Are they in line with your golden vision?

- Do some more work on the push–pull balancing exercise on p. 93.

- Commit to changing your perspective on the restraining forces currently operating in your life, and look for the positive opportunities they present.

Detail

- Ensure you have identified all the objectives and tasks required for each change you intend to make in your life (see Dream Exercise 3 on p. 92).

- Allocate an achievable time-frame to each of these objectives and tasks.

- Make a calendar to check how you are doing on your deadlines and to motivate yourself to stay on track.

- Revisit each of your vision statements and see how you can make them more colourful, inspirational and specific.

- Do the five whys exercise for any activity you are undertaking today to check that it is consistent with your core values.

Change

- Take an existing habit – even if it's just the time you usually get up in the mornings – and break it. Do something differently today.

- Commit to looking at today's 'mistakes' as invaluable learning points on your journey to success.

- Review your objectives and tasks, and take action on something before you were due to.

- Look at what you are procrastinating over. Take a deep breath – and do it.

- Review your wardrobe, colour scheme and hair style. If your external appearance isn't in line with the new person you are becoming, bring the future forward a little and change it.

Intuition

- Be attuned to how you feel about a person or situation today, rather than just what logic is telling you.

- Commit to opening yourself up to Divine Guidance through 'hunches'. Count the number of times your intuition nudges you today, even if you don't choose to act on any of them.

- Write one or more affirmations to underscore a positive attitude towards intuition.

- Act on an intuitive urge, keeping in mind the Wiccan philosophy: 'If it harms none, do what you will.'

- Explore your beliefs about intuition. Which explanation – if you feel any is needed – are you most comfortable with? Where do you think intuition 'comes from'?

Diversity

- Today, commit to asking five people: 'Can you help me . . .?' and listen to their advice.

- Go and say hello to your mystery mentor(s). What challenge might they help you with today?

- Find one positive characteristic that you admire in at least one of the people you meet today. Ask them, 'How do you do that?'

- When faced with a difficult decision, ask your mystery mentor: 'What do you know about this that I have missed?'

- Commit to accepting that other people have different ways of looking at the world than you. Without judgement or comment, listen to their perspectives on a topic you feel strongly about. Then try to find more things that you can accept about their viewpoint than you choose to dismiss.

Detachment

- Today, commit to detaching from one specific outcome and the desire to control events so that it occurs exactly as you want it to. Wait, instead, to see what the universe conjures up.

- Review your current love relationship, or other important partnership, and look for ways in which you can, as the poet Kahlil Gibran puts it, 'allow the winds of heaven to dance between you'.

- Look at one area of your life in which you are experiencing frustration, unhappiness, pain or fear. Explore the extent to which it is not the situation but your controlling attitude that is causing the problem.

- Become an alien for a day (see Detach Exercise 2 on p. 139).

- Decide to regard delays, frustrations and non-action

as 'white space', full of creative potential. Be comfortable with the void. Remember, life abhors a vacuum.
Determine to be patient to see what fills it.

The following three stories highlight how other heroic
travellers have ventured into the labyrinth and enhanced
their lives as a result.

CASE HISTORY: Jack's Story

Having always focused on choosing staff according to their
skills, qualifications and experience, Jack was finding not
only that his team of highly paid employees was not functioning effectively together but that customer satisfaction
levels had plummeted. His vision was to establish a 'dream
team' of highly motivated, high-EQ individuals with the same
passion, entrepreneurial spirit and regard for customer service as himself. A single man with no dependants, Jack's
business was his 'baby' and he had derived much satisfaction from its success.

Throughout and after walking the Dream pathways,
Jack established that there was a significant chasm
between how his business needed to operate and the way
it was currently being run. However, given that it would
have been commercial suicide to get rid of everyone and
start from scratch, Jack used the concept of detail to establish two lists – the competencies required of each role in his
company, and the individual skills and personal interests of
each employee. He immediately saw where the gaps
between the two lists were most acute and committed to
changing his recruitment and motivation policy. Jack also
recognised that, had he acted on his intuition rather than
on what he read on paper, he might never have employed
certain individuals for the jobs they now filled.

While looking for ways in which to overcome his staffing
problems, Jack came across a US business magazine with
which he wasn't familiar. Flicking through it, he found an
article about a much larger company than his that had
completely restructured itself with few, if any, redundancies.

Having already established a mystery mentor committee of various management gurus, Jack e-mailed the CEO of the American company and received a detailed reply on how they had handled their employee shake-up.

Although habitually task-driven and with a need to dot every 'i' and cross every 't', Jack decided to put some slack into his restructuring procedure in order to be flexible enough to respond to new information and feedback from his staff. Jack's central labyrinthine symbol had been a gold cup with the number one inscribed on it, such as a football team might win. He had automatically thought it to be a sporting trophy and joked that he was obviously destined to win the local amateur golfing championship. But with the right people at last in the right positions in his business, Jack found a different relevance for it as sales figures escalated and his company climbed back on top.

CASE HISTORY: Joanna's Story

Joanna had a long history of short-term relationships with dysfunctional men, many of whom were married and had no intention of leaving their wives and children for her. Although at ease with her single status, she began to question whether she would ever attract a balanced, loving, mutually supportive partner.

On Pathway 1, she 'saw' her soul-mate as an Arthurian knight frequently away on various quests, who was brave, exciting, different and very much her equal. The labyrinth experience motivated Joanna to think not only about the kind of man she wanted as a partner, but also about the nature of the relationship. She recognised that there was little about her lifestyle that she wanted to change since she had a wide circle of friends and a vibrant social life. Intuitively she was drawn to a particular Internet dating service where she found the profile of what sounded like her ideal man – in Boston, Massachusetts. But this was not too much of a problem since Joanna visited the east coast of the US on business every six to eight weeks.

Although his cultural background was very different

from her own, her meeting with Ray highlighted many shared values and goals. She had been very controlling within relationships in the past and had alienated a number of potential partners by bombarding them with phone calls and e-mails, but the labyrinthine process had taught Joanna to trust that if Ray was 'The One' then everything would turn out just fine – without her help. She and Ray communicated infrequently between meetings, but on each occasion they met their respect and affection for each other grew.

While neither wishes to uproot themselves at the moment, Joanna feels she has found the committed relationship she longed for – without the disadvantages of a full-time, live-in arrangement. Her labyrinth symbol had been a passion flower. Joanna tells me she is of the firm opinion that prolonged passion – an essential part of any relationship for her – can only be maintained when lovers keep a certain amount of situational distance between them. Finally she had discovered that she didn't need to be a mistress in order to achieve that.

CASE HISTORY: Michael's Story

Michael's life was a mess. Fearful about doing the wrong thing, he continually put off important decisions, alienating his colleagues at work and frustrating his family and friends. Known as 'mouse-like Mike', this obviously talented, likeable young man had stalled on his life path. He was also constantly in debt because he ignored bills and was afraid of facing up to the fact that his income was far short of his outgoings.

Michael's vision for his life proved, not surprisingly, to be nebulous. All he could 'see' on his screen was blue sky dotted with fluffy clouds and the occasional hovering bird. He told me that since tension, detail and change seemed interminable constants in his life, he simply wanted the freedom to be like a bird, with no worries or cares whatsoever.

While Michael's intuition was well-developed, his downfall had come from not acting on the many inspirational hunches he had been given throughout his life. His mystery mentor was an Aztec sun god called Quetzalcoatl, whose appearance turned out to be remarkably like Michael's – tall, with pale skin, long dark hair (which Michael kept tied in a ponytail at work) and a beard. When a brochure arrived at his home offering long trekking and camping holidays in the Yucatan peninsula of Mexico, Michael was struck by the desire to resign his junior management position, pay off his credit cards, borrow a little from his parents and go off for four months into the unknown. For once he took action based on this almost unshakeable need to be some place else.

Michael felt deeply at home in Mexico. An avid reader of ancient history and mythology, he proved to be very knowledgeable about the sacred sites and temples that his group visited. He was regarded as such an asset that a couple of the American tour leaders agreed to put in a good word for him and he applied for a similar job with their company.

Every so often I get a postcard from Michael, somewhere in Central or North America. He is at last experiencing the freedom his soul was crying out for and, although the job pays very little, all his expenses are covered so that he no longer has to concern himself with personal finances.

Michael had been disappointed to find that imaginatively submerging himself in the labyrinth pool had uncovered nothing more symbolic than the clear, still water itself. But since he was a young man overwhelmed by the pressures of a materialistic lifestyle he so patently disliked, I think that fluidity is entirely appropriate as a representation of his new life.

And Finally. . . .

Even though this book deals with a lot of spiritual concepts I have attempted to make it as practical and down-to-earth as possible, including scientific explanations for esoteric experiences wherever relevant. However, I would like to end by relating a scene from that wonderful film *Shakespeare in Love* starring Gwyneth Paltrow and Joseph Fiennes. In it Philip Henslowe, the owner of London's Rose theatre and a man who always manages to avoid the detritus being thrown in his path, is talking to his creditors about the impending disaster facing the business. Even though Henslowe says there is nothing they can do about it, he assures the others that everything will turn out well. When asked how, he replies: 'I don't know, it's a mystery.'

I would urge you to approach life in a similar way. It is not always possible to explain exactly why things turn out as they do. Just remember that not getting what you want precisely as and when you want it usually turns out to be a marvellous stroke of luck in retrospect. Trust that the universe is taking care of the details. And trust, too, that you are a magnificent, unique, value-creating individual who has many attributes that don't need changing in any way at all.

No matter how imperfect things seem at the moment, everything in your life is unfolding as it should, in its own time, in its own way. And the universe, even at this moment, is conspiring to help you find fulfilment. So enjoy the continuing journey by focusing on the scenery and not on your destination. You'll get to where you're meant to be, believe me.

APPENDIX:

THE LABYRINTHINE JOURNEY – GUIDED VISUALISATION

This is the guided visualisation that you will listen to on tape as you make your journey into your personal labyrinth. The only thing to remember now is to be fully present in the experience, take your time over it, focus on your breathing – and enjoy this wonderful, life-changing adventure.

Close your eyes. Make sure you are in a relaxed position, and that any stray thoughts entering your head that are not relevant to the labyrinthine process are acknowledged but allowed to float by like a fish in a stream. You cannot ignore the fact that the fish is there, but you can choose how much you focus on it. Remember, your focus is on the journey you are about to take . . . an exciting adventure into the depths of your being . . . the culmination of which will be accessing your Divine Potential and finding the fulfilment that you deserve in your life. Remember to breathe evenly and deeply, relaxing your body more and more with every breath you take . . . breathing out all tension and physical aches and pains with every exhalation.

You are standing at the mouth of your labyrinth. . . . You are light and free with only the clothes on your body and bare feet that connect you to the ground. . . . Take four steps forward so that you are surrounded on three sides – left, right and in front – by the walls of your labyrinth. Take a moment to bring to mind what your labyrinth is like. . . . Is the temperature warm or cool? . . . Are the walls damp or dry? . . . What decoration, if any, is on them? . . . Look down, in your mind's eye, at the floor. . . . What is it made of? . . . What does it feel like? . . . Smooth or rough? . . . Wet or dry? . . . What colour are the floor, the walls, the ceiling? . . . Is there a fragrance in your labyrinth? . . . If so, silently put a name to it. . . . Begin to walk ahead a little until you reach the wall in front of you. . . . What sounds do your footsteps make? . . . Is there an echo in your labyrinth? . . .

Now turn to your left and begin walking into Pathway 1 . . . it is illuminated, making your labyrinth a safe, comfortable, exciting place to be for you at this time. . . .

As you walk along this, the first of the Dream pathways, become aware that the wall to your right is covered with a screen. On the floor by your feet is a remote control handset. Press the big red button on the handset now. This allows you to watch your current life projected five, ten, fifteen years or more from now. . . . This story is the result of the present course you have set your life on . . . the result of the current choices you are making. . . . You are watching where your relationship with your partner is heading . . . your career path . . . the people who are in your life including children . . . members of your extended family . . . and friends. . . . You are aware of your future health . . . your financial situation . . . where you are living. . . . At any time you can press the pause button to concentrate on any particular scene. . . .

(Pause for ten seconds.)

As you watch this future life, the extension of the path

you are currently on . . . be aware of any discomfort in your mind or body related to any of these areas. . . . You have the power to change your future in any way you desire. . . . That power is in your hands right now. . . . Be aware that you can fade out any part of this future that you do not wish to happen. . . . And, by pressing another button on your handset marked 'New Future', you can change that scene to whatever is most desirable to you and in keeping with the wisdom of your Higher Self. . . . Do this now. . . .

(Pause for ten seconds.)

Now it's time to turn round another bend into the next pathway . . . the pathway of tension. . . . The walls of this second pathway curve gently from right to left. . . . Take a deep breath. . . . Smell the fragrant, fresh air. . . . Feel the floor beneath your feet. . . . Be aware of your labyrinth through your all senses. . . .

Be aware that you have come to an invisible, flexible force field. . . . This represents your comfort zone. . . . Think again about all the ways in which you wish your vision of the future to be different from the projection of the current path you viewed on the screen in Pathway 1. . . . How do you wish it to be the same? . . . Just be aware of any feeling of tension between where you are now and where you want to be . . . the discomfort you feel about the way your current life is progressing. . . . Whether you are motivated away from the past and the present or towards the future doesn't matter. . . . You are fired up by the desire to change certain aspects of your life so that they become different from the current course it is on.

Hold that feeling as you push against the force field . . . your comfort zone. . . . How resistant is it? . . . Become aware of some of the specific differences between the life you have and the life you want. . . . The future you deserve is magnetic and compelling. . . . You are breaking through that force field. . . . Now . . . on to a new, more empowering and fulfilling course. . . .

(Pause for ten seconds.)

You are entering Pathway 3, which covers the entire perimeter of your labyrinth . . . there is no need to rush. . . . Take time to consider some of the changes you need to make in order to bring your ideal life, a life of total fulfilment, into your current reality. . . .

Think about where you are now and what you need to commit yourself to doing to steer yourself firmly through the new course you have chosen. . . . What new attitudes, beliefs, behaviours and values do you now have to embrace to bring that about? . . . Briefly jot down any ideas that come to you. . . .

(Pause.)

Now imagine these new attitudes, beliefs, behaviours and values, and this fresh sense of purpose, as a cloak lying on the floor of your labyrinth. . . . When you are ready, put it on . . . and move ever closer to your new destiny. . . .

(Pause for ten seconds.)

Now it's time to enter the first of the Do pathways . . . Pathway 4 . . . the pathway of change. . . . Because the purpose of this pathway is concerned with changing behaviour, think about one thing you will commit to doing differently today . . . right now . . . that will begin to make your most fulfilled future a reality. . . . There is no need to wait until you have effectively changed your thoughts before you take this action. . . . Ask your Higher Self what it is you need to do to make that change a reality . . . now. . . .

(Pause for ten seconds.)

You will shortly be coming to the entrance to Pathway 5. . . . This is the shortest pathway. . . . Slow yourself down as you come to it. . . . Be aware of your breathing. . . . Relax your body and mind even more deeply as you move further into the labyrinth. . . . Imagine that in the middle of this short pathway is a puddle of water. . . . What does it feel like to run your finger through this tiny pool? . . . Imagine you are looking into the dark water. . . . Your reflection is looking back at you as you ask: 'What do I need to know to overcome the challenges between where I am and where I am meant to be? . . . What do I know about my mission in life that I thought I didn't know?' . . . The fluidity of this puddle of water offers a flash of inspiration, a gut feeling, a creative hunch that is relevant to your journey. . . . You are aware of it now. . . .

(Pause for ten seconds.)

Be clear about what intuition you have been offered before you move on . . . slipping into Pathway 6 – the pathway of diversity. . . .

In this sixth pathway, which is slightly longer but slopes even more deeply downwards than the last, you become aware of a shrouded figure. . . . This is your mystery mentor . . . someone whose attitude, behaviour, gifts, life history . . . are a source of inspiration to you. . . . Who is this person? . . . Male or female . . . it could be someone you know or do not know . . . someone living or not living. . . . Be aware of them . . . now. . . .

(Pause for ten seconds.)

As you begin to enter the seventh pathway . . . you are aware of the need to be open to new, as yet unknown possibilities. . . . This is the first of the Detach pathways, representing the ability to let go, to detach from specific outcomes and allow the universe to take care of the details of your life for you. . . . You are stepping into the unknown with trust and the belief that your life is just as you desire it to be. . . . Imagine your quantum self as a brilliant golden light that penetrates and is penetrated by everything that has ever been, is, or ever will be. . . . You are an intrinsic part of the Divine Plan . . . one facet of the cosmic web . . . an invaluable thread in the pattern of life. . . . Be aware of your potential . . . the potential that comes from your connection with all things in the universe. . . . Take a moment to enjoy that sense of energy . . . of no longer being bounded by a body . . . free from the limitations of your physical self.

(Pause for ten seconds.)

Move forwards now . . . towards the centre of the

labyrinth where a special gift awaits you . . . a symbolic gift from your Higher Self. . . .

Close your eyes, if you have not already done so. . . . In your mind's eye see, in the centre of this special place, a small pool. . . . It is not gated or walled but open as it merges with the stones on the floor of the labyrinth. The water is still and very, very deep. Within this pool lie many different objects with which seekers find the answer to whatever they are looking for. Imagine you are looking into the dark, shiny water and see your reflection staring back at you. . . . Feel your hand skim across the top of the water, letting the droplets trickle through your fingers. . . . The water is pleasantly warm. . . . It smells sweetly of flowers or herbs. . . . Now plunge your arm, your face or your whole body into the water – whichever you choose. . . . The pool is deep but safe, there is no current and you can come back to the surface any time you like. . . . There is an object, a symbol – something in the water that can help you with whatever challenge at this moment faces you. . . . This is the key to finding fulfilment in your life. . . . Go into the water now and bring it out.

(Pause for ten seconds.)

Look at your object. . . . Turn it round so you can see it from all angles. . . . Feel it, make a note of any colour. . . . Be clear about what it is but don't be concerned about what it means at this moment, unless you have an immediate insight. . . .

(Short pause.)

Now it's time to come out of the labyrinth. Place the object back into the water for someone else to find. . . . And open your eyes. . . .

You now have all the treasure you need to lead a life of self-fulfilment, to become complete and whole and fulfil your life's mission. . . . As you retrace your steps through the labyrinth, in silence, and with the pathways imprinted in your mind's eye, think about all the gifts you have been offered. . . . Consider the connection between them . . .

what pattern they suggest. . . . How you might use them to best effect in your life. . . . In a moment there will be only the names and numbers of the pathways in reverse order, followed by silence or gentle background music as you make your way out of your labyrinth . . . the single road that led you in . . . as it will lead you out. . . . Take your time over this final part of the process. . . . Leave the centre of your labrinth now and move into. . . .

Pathway 7 – where you discovered your energetic Self, the Self that is without physical form and hence boundaries. . . .

(Pause.)

Pathway 6 – where you came upon your mystery mentor . . . someone whose life will act as a constant source of inspiration and wisdom. . . .

(Pause.)

Pathway 5 – where you received the gift of intuition, the flashes of inspiration that are always available to you and which represent your innate homing device for success. . . .

(Pause.)

Pathway 4 – in which you committed to one specific change in your behaviour and hence to redirect the course of your life. . . .

(Pause.)

Pathway 3 – where you considered all the little details of the changes that you will implement to make your future life even more of a reality. . . .

(Pause.)

Pathway 2 – where you acutely sensed the tension between the life you have and the life you are meant to lead. . . .

(Pause.)

And Pathway 1 – the video showing what your life will be like if you continue on the path you are travelling now. . . .

(Pause.)

Now you have reached the mouth of your imaginary

labyrinth. . . . Take a moment to become aware of the room which you are currently in . . . open your eyes, if they are closed, stretch your arms and legs . . . take a drink or light snack and gradually reorient yourself.

Congratulations. . . . The first part of your journey is over. . . . Now it's time to work with the insights offered to you by your Higher Self . . . and to learn how to use them in your life so that every day is as fulfilling, enthusiastic and centred as you would like it to be.

USEFUL ADDRESSES

The following organisations offer more information about labyrinths and their use as a spiritual and personal development tool. They can help you to locate church or public labyrinths for walking and to find out about labyrinth tours, and offer instructions and advice on how to construct your own, permanent outdoor labyrinth or how to buy or make a portable labyrinth for personal use.

Labyrinthos

53 Thundersley Grove, Thundersley, Essex, SS7 3EB, UK
Website: www.labyrinthos.net
E-mail: jeff@labyrinthos.net

Labyrinthos is a non-profit organisation that provides a focus for the study of mazes and labyrinths. It publishes an annual journal called *Caerdroia, the Journal of Mazes and Labyrinths*, which contains news, theories and findings about these subjects, as well as distributing a range of labyrinthine publications and products. Publisher Jeff Saward also maintains a directory of individuals, businesses and organisations related to mazes and labyrinths. A wonderful resource for anyone further interested in these fascinating spiritual tools.

Mid-Atlantic Geomancy

Website: www.geomancy.org

The website of spiritual ecologist and labyrinth expert Sig Lonegren. The homepage link to Mid-Atlantic Geomancy includes much invaluable information and advice on labyrinths, including how to make a labyrinth; where they are found; locating a site for your permanent labyrinth; and laying out an outdoor labyrinth. Highly recommended.

Veriditas and the Grace Cathedral Labyrinth Project

Website: www.gracecathedral.org/labyrinth/locator/index. shtml

An opportunity to discover the location of a permanent or canvas Chartres-type labyrinth close to where you live. Although principally offering US locations, some UK labyrinths are mentioned. The main Grace Cathedral website (www.gracecathedral.org) also offers a collection of inspirational messages from the Revd Dr Lauren Artress, the Canon for Special Ministries and creator of the Labyrinth Project. These include details of how walking these sacred pathways has helped people bring about their own psycho-spiritual healing. Grace Cathedral in San Francisco, US, has two labyrinths, one of which is an outdoor stone terrazzo labyrinth that is available to the public for walking twenty-four hours a day, seven days a week. The other is a canvas labyrinth. Internet surfers can experience a 'virtual tour' of both labyrinths on-line.

The Labyrinth Project

128 Slocum Avenue, St Louis, MO 63119 2254, US
Tel: (314) 968 5557 or (800) 873 9873
Fax: (314) 968 5539 or (888) 873 9873
Website: www.labyrinthproject.com

The director of the Labyrinth Project, Robert Ferré, has made his living as a labyrinth-maker since 1996 and claims to be the most prolific maker of labyrinths in the world. He and his three assistants are called upon to supply canvas, permanent outdoor and temporary labyrinths ranging from 20 feet to 104 feet in diameter. The Labyrinth Project has supplied all the canvas labyrinths sold via Veriditas and the Grace Cathedral Labyrinth Project (see above) to churches across the US. Ferré is also founder and tour director of One Heart Tours, a personalised tour company specialising in pilgrimage to sacred sites in France, including Chartres Cathedral.

The Labyrinth Society (TLS)

PO Box 144, New Canaan, CT 06840–0144, US
Tel: 877 446 4520
Website: www.labyrinthsociety.org
E-mail: labsociety@aol.com

This is a newly formed global society whose mission is to 'support all those who create, maintain and use labyrinths and to serve the global community by providing education, networking and opportunities to experience transformation'. Webpages include: What is a labyrinth?; events; membership; and how to make a labyrinth. The society also offers links to other useful labyrinth organisations and Internet sites, including labyrinth-makers.

Liz Simpson

If you would like further information about Liz Simpson's work, particularly her personal coaching sessions, workshops, motivational talks and forthcoming, interactive Labyrinth website, please write to her c/o Piatkus Books, E-mail: info@heartwork.com; or visit her website: www.heartwork.com

FURTHER READING

Labyrinths

Artress, Dr Lauren, *Walking a Sacred Path: Rediscovering the Labyrinth as a Spiritual Tool*, Riverhead Books, 1995

Attali, Jacques, *The Labyrinth in Culture and Society*, North Atlantic Books, 1999

Lonegren, Sig, *Labyrinths: Ancient Myths and Modern Uses*, Gothic Image Publications, 1991, 1996

Matthews, W. H., *Mazes and Labyrinths: Their History and Development*, Dover Publications, 1970

The Goddess Within

Bolen, Jean Shinoda, *Goddesses in Everywoman: A New Psychology of Women*, HarperCollins, 1985

Curott, Phyllis W., *Book of Shadows*, Piatkus Books, 1998

Self-Development

Breathnach, Sarah Ban, *Simple Abundance: A Daybook of Comfort and Joy*, Bantam Press, 1996

Chopra, Deepak, *The Seven Spiritual Laws of Success: A Practical Guide to the Fulfilment of your Dreams*, Amber-Allen Publishing, 1994

Robbins, Anthony, *Awaken the Giant Within*, Simon & Schuster, 1992

Simpson, Liz, *Working from the Heart: A Practical Guide to Loving What You Do for a Living*, Vermilion, 1999

Walsh, Roger, *Essential Spirituality: The Seven Central Practices to Awaken Heart and Mind*, John Wiley and Sons, 1999

General

Capra, Fritof, *The Turning Point*, Flamingo, 1983

Colgan, Dr Michael, *The New Nutrition: Medicine for the Millenium*, Apple Publishing, 1995

Holford, Patrick, *The Optimum Nutrition Bible*, Piatkus, 1997

Hunt, Valerie V., *Infinite Mind: The Science of Human Vibrations*, Malibu Publishing Co. (US), 1995

Kenton, Leslie, *The New Joy of Beauty*, Vermilion, 1995

Lawlor, Robert, *Sacred Geometry: Philosophy and Practice*, Thames and Hudson, 1982

Swan, James A. (ed.), *The Power of Place*, Gateway Books, 1993

INDEX